The *Digital* Marketing Strategy PLAYBOOK

The cheat code for a planned and profitable digital presence

TISHA HOLMAN

ISBN: 979-8-218-88343-0

DEDICATION

To Sydney Alexandria,
Your kind heart, laughter, and brilliance remind me every day why legacy matters. You are the blueprint for every brave step I take.

To the extraordinary souls who inspired Dora Marchérie,
Thank you for the heritage and heart behind this journey.

And to the small business owners and leaders who wake up every day determined to create work that honors their gifts and build a legacy rooted in both meaning and abundance--This book is for you.

May it be the catalyst for success, clarity, and the impact you were destined to make on the world.

CONTENTS

Revenue & Reach 136

Execution 182

PULLING IT ALL TOGETHER 232

CONTENTS

FOREWORD

What does it require for one to make it in today's world? Einstein said, "The thinking that has brought us this far has created some problems that this thinking can't solve". There are certain things you need to possess if you are going to beat the odds and live a life that matters. You have to think differently and be the kind of person who makes things happen. First, you have to be an innovator. In today's entrepreneurial climate, businesses have gone from brick and mortar to click and order so you have to be unafraid to stand out and make things happen. Here's something else. You have to care about and have a heart for people. Are you that person who is willing to go the extra mile for others? It was Maya Angelou who said, "People don't care what you know, until they know how much you care." If someone just needs information, they can go online and "Google" it - the truth is, people do not buy into programs; they buy into people. It is one thing to be heard, but it is something else to be felt. Your brand is your story, and you've got to tell it to the world…strategically. Next, you have to have tenacity. There will be all kinds of things that will happen and interrupt your life - what are you going to do about it? You have to snatch victory from the jaws of defeat and be one of the people who is going to take a stand and make a decision - make a mark in this world; those are the ones who are going to win. Finally, you have to have spiritual strength. You can have all the motivation in the world, but the real power comes in knowing who you are and whose you are. Greater is He that is in you than he that is in the world. When you have spiritual strength, oh, it doesn't mean that things aren't going to happen to you.

It doesn't mean that every day is going to be a good day. But here is what it does mean - It means that there is some good in every day. People who know about spiritual strength understand that all things work together for the good of those who love God and for those who are called according to His purpose.

Are you going to be the one who is tenacious, flexible, versatile, and adaptable in incorporating digital marketing strategies that will take them in the direction of what they want to achieve? Because at the end of the day, you will fail your way to success. There will be challenges, setbacks, and a lot of things that you don't see coming, which is why you must understand that you cannot do this by yourself. In order to make it, you are going to need to create a team of collaborative, achievement-driven, supportive people. You are going to need to build a community with people you can grow with and learn from. As Sidney Poitier, Academy Award-winning actor, said, "When you go for a walk with someone, something happens without being spoken. Either they adjust to your pace, or you adjust to their pace." Whose pace have you adjusted to?

So much has changed, and the people who will make it in this place are the people who understand that there are new rules. This new level where we are requires new skills and new strategies; new input and thinking that can take you beyond where you are right now. And through tenacity, caring, building strong relationships, spiritual strength, and being an innovator - Staying ahead of technology, learning all you can, and expanding your vision of yourself for what's possible - you can beat the odds. Only 8 out of 100 people who started out with resolutions at the beginning of the year are going to succeed because they followed the steps I just shared with you.

In The Digital Marketing Strategy Playbook, you will uncover the hidden gems you need to beat the odds and experience success that others won't, simply because they are unwilling to put in the work. Tisha Holman is giving you the proven framework, the cheat code if you will, that will quickly take you in the direction of what you want to achieve. In conversing with Tisha, I learned that her character and ability to remain faithful to strategies and systems are born in the wisdom gleaned from her dear grandmother, Arline Holman. Affectionately known as Nana, this woman has indelibly left her stamp on Tisha, and it is what has driven her to this day. If you ask someone, "What is Tisha like?" They will say she is driven, she has tenacity, and she cares about others. She comes from a strong spiritual foundation, and she is an innovator - she can come up with a strategy that can take your stuff out into the stratosphere.

If you want to beat the odds, do not just say that you will; have a strategy that will make your plan a reality. The Digital Marketing Strategy Playbook is the answer you have been looking for. Take in every ounce of advice that you read in this book and apply it! You cannot and will not fail if you simply use this tool created just for you!

Les Brown

Introduction

If you are reading this book, you are either looking for answers or you want to inch a little closer towards discovering them. Entrepreneurs and business owners do not have it easy in today's digital marketplace. The pressure to stand out on social media is more than a notion. But many don't consider what happens after they get the followers. Too often, the planning stops at the posts. Do you find yourself asking: how are businesses turning "likes" into cash? What is the cheat code for going viral online? Perhaps you identify with knowing that you are sitting on a gold mine of a business, but you feel stuck because it is not taking off like you thought it would — or should have??

I have encountered many business owners who feel like their passion is enough to bring in a profit. If I'm being honest, that was me once upon a time (more on that later). Many assume that potential clients will see what they are offering and be just as excited to buy as they are to sell. I hate to be the bearer of bad news, but it just does not work that way.

Would it surprise you that only 23% of small businesses owners have a strategy for what they do online? To be fair, I don't think that most people recognize the need for a strategy online. Going viral, trending, or becoming an "overnight" success looks almost accidental from the outside. In the absence of a strategy, many do what they see those who they perceive to be successful doing online. Does any of this sound familiar?

While we are on the subject, you would be shocked to learn how many "Wizard of Oz" influencers, coaches, and brands are out here on these digital highways and byways, just faking it until they make it —kind of like you, without a strategy or a plan. They are branded and packaged well, touting the recipe for the secret sauce to your success, but their stuff is just as jacked up as yours, held together with duct tape, a wing, and a prayer. You may never make it behind the curtain to see the disappointing reality that your favorite "Wizard" really needs a little help too, but hopefully, you do make it to the end of this book and become a better, more strategic business owner in all the ways you can.

My most sincere desire is that business owners recognize the necessity of a strategy and all that comes along with it —even in the presence of evolving technologies. There has to be a strategy that goes above and beyond the plan. There have to be intentional, calculated steps that make success predictable for your organization. Doing what you have always done won't be enough in this season if you are truly wanting to scale your business and get beyond just "owning a job. "Did I strike a nerve? The next level of success is waiting for you, but you have to start doing next-level stuff to get there. Climb into the "trust tree" with me. The pages of this book are going to change the game for you, that is, if you are willing to put in the work.

I like to think the CORE™ Model is the very thing that every entrepreneur and business owner is waiting for in order to take their business and life to the next level. I have poured it all out on these pages for you.

This is MY playbook.

The nuggets, gems, and life-changing tactics on the following pages are exactly what I have used to:

- Craft strategies that propelled social media followings over the million mark in less than a year.
- Take books to the top of the New York Times bestseller list.
- Launch movies that premiered with record-breaking ratings and became national trending topics.
- Successfully "handle" viral digital conundrums with the same skill and finesse of our favorite gladiator Olivia Pope.
- Help build the brands of some of our most endeared public figures.
- Enable global conferences to impact their audiences in deeper more meaningful ways, while also increasing profits and reach.

But what I am most proud of, is the work I have done with brave entrepreneurs like you.

Just to give you a heads up, I am an acronym generating machine, and you will see quite a bit of it in the pages that follow. It helps me organize my thoughts and distill concepts that can have a lot of moving parts—hopefully it does the same for you. The CORE™ Model is proven, tried, and true.

And now it's yours.

The digital space is your oyster. The beauty of this playbook and The CORE™ Model is that it releases you from winging it online and throwing content on the walls of your social feeds to see if it will stick. Gone are the days of you relying on friends and family to support what you are doing (they probably aren't your ideal client anyway, but we'll talk more about that later). It's time to ditch that thirsty sales energy you put out there when you need jusssst enough money to cover a bill. No more grinding, because that is what gears do when they are out of alignment. It's exhausting. There is something greater out there for you and the people you are called to serve, and that is why I'm sharing my playbook with you.

No quick fixes, no fluff, no lofty promises. All I have to offer you is truth and a shift in your thinking that will lead you to the perks of being properly prepared in the digital space. I want you to feel above and beyond confident when you hit the ground running, because by the time you get to the end of this book, you will hit the ground running towards success.

If you are ready to lay the foundation and build a planned, positioned, purposeful, and profitable business in the digital space, I've got the tools you need to build a brand that will take you to the next level!

"When your strategy is aligned, your brand becomes unstoppable."

Tisha Holman

When I founded Mind Your Business, I felt a strong responsibility to make sure I was helping the businesses I served build a strategy that was a solid foundation, based on real principles, that would elevate their success in a sustainable way. I saw so many others in my industry providing trendy tactics with no mention of a real strategy, and I wanted to be different. I knew that I wanted to be known as the digital marketing strategist who worked with serious-minded individuals, not those looking for a microwave solution and vanity metrics. Success online is so much more than trending topics and viral videos. If you do this correctly, your online presence becomes a well-oiled machine that frees you up to thrive in areas of your business that are being neglected instead of a source of stress, frustration and burnout because you don't have any viable leads coming through the door. Of course, through research, trial & error, and a keen awareness of evolution in the digital space, the signature proprietary process I used to help my clients transform their business has itself evolved throughout the years into something that I am so proud to share with you today. I have learned, you don't necessarily need to do more or post more online—you just need to do the right things consistently. Although it may appear daunting on the surface, I promise you that careful and dedicated navigation through each step of the process will prove to be one of the best decisions you have ever made for yourself and your business.

Allow me to introduce you to The C.O.R.E.™ Model.

The C.O.R.E. Model™

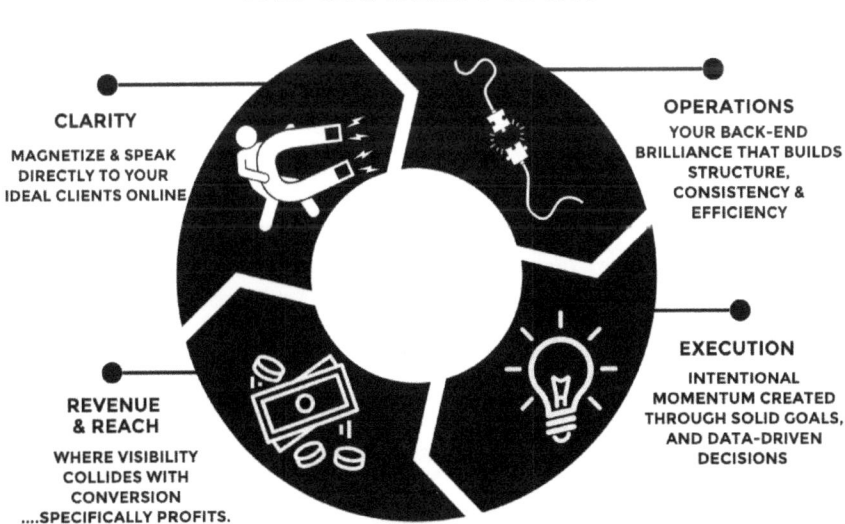

CLARITY
MAGNETIZE & SPEAK DIRECTLY TO YOUR IDEAL CLIENTS ONLINE

OPERATIONS
YOUR BACK-END BRILLIANCE THAT BUILDS STRUCTURE, CONSISTENCY & EFFICIENCY

EXECUTION
INTENTIONAL MOMENTUM CREATED THROUGH SOLID GOALS, AND DATA-DRIVEN DECISIONS

REVENUE & REACH
WHERE VISIBILITY COLLIDES WITH CONVERSION ....SPECIFICALLY PROFITS.

THE FOUR-PART FOUNDATION BEHIND EVERY PROFITABLE AND POSITIONED ONLINE PRESENCE.

Clarity

Operations

Revenue/Reach

Execution

These simple, yet powerful elements organize the most critical pieces of your business, and are what will ultimately make you a formidable presence in your industry and a generator of legacy-building wealth. Every part of your business is connected, and The C.O.R.E.™ Model makes sure your messaging, marketing, operations, and systems aren't siloed. Before we begin building out the elements of The C.O.R.E. Model for your business, let me explain the model in more detail.

Clarity

This is where our work begins. This is the step where the slate is wiped clean, and any perceptions you have had about your digital marketing presence that have been holding you back are addressed. This is where you really dig deep and get to know the client you are targeting so you can begin to share content that will have them stuck to you like glue. Everybody and every brand has a story; this is where we develop yours. Without a strong sense of clarity, everything else about your digital marketing will be like tires stuck in mud trying to spin their way to freedom—good luck with that my friend. The Clarity stage ensures that your audience knows exactly what you do, who you serve, and why you are unequivocally the best one to do it.

The results of the Clarity stage are going to magnetize the right people and repel the wrong ones. You will get to experience the exhilaration of what it is like to "vibe with your tribe".

I can tell you from experience, there is something truly special about the moment when you realize you are in your zone of genius and the very audience you want to serve is dialed into what you are sharing with them. Clarity is what eliminates confusion—for you, your team, and your audience. You were given a set of gifts and talents, and it's those very gifts and talents that you then must give away to the world - and that is the beauty of the Clarity stage: alignment.

Key Components:

> Mindset Matters
>
> Market Research
>
> The Digital Audit
>
> The Perfect M.A.T.C.H.
>
> Get B.R.A.N.D.E.D.
>
> Creating Your CopySignature™

Operations

Author Michael E. Gerber said, "If your business needs you to run it, you don't own a business, you own a job." If you can't say amen to that, just say ouch! Every business owner has been in this place; it is a rite of passage of sorts.

However, if your business is ever going to truly grow and scale to a place where you are truly the CEO of your business, you have to structure your operations in a way that prepares you to build a team that can deliver the same quality of service that clients receive from you, in your absence. I remember my very first job—McDonald's. One of the fascinating things about McDonald's is the training and onboarding process. If you are not already familiar, as a part of the marketing campaign for the 1996 Olympic Games in Atlanta, GA McDonald's released a jazzy rendition of the popular Big Mac© jingle sung by Al Jarreau and Vesta Williams called the "Big Mac© Scat" (check it out on YouTube). You know the words, right? "Two all-beef patties, special sauce, lettuce, cheese, pickles, onions, on a sesame seed bun…". This description of the trademark menu offering is more than a catchy tune; it is also the actual order of ingredients in the preparation of Big Mac© 's in every restaurant. Extensive focus groups and testing determined this order to be the tastiest version. What an ingenious concept! This allows McDonald's—where billions are served daily—to offer a replicable, consistent product no matter which location you visit. Your goal in the Operations stage is similar: to create, test, and document guidelines, policies, and procedures for employee training and development. When people join your organization, they will learn what you do, how to do it, and have clear expectations outlined in carefully written policies.

This is your back-end brilliance—how your digital marketing strategy will run with structure, consistency, and efficiency.

It is where you curate systems that support delegation, implement tech that enhances efficiency & makes dollars and sense, and leverage data and real metrics that impact your bottom line. Operations is the part of the C.O.R.E.™ Model where you turn your brand into a business, stop being the bottleneck in broken processes, and begin to scale with integrity.

Key Components:

> Policies
>
> Standard Operating Procedures (SOPs)
>
> Key Performance Indicators (KPIs)
>
> Monitoring & Frequently Asked Questions
>
> Crisis Management
>
> Hiring Right

Reach & Revenue

The Reach & Revenue stage of the model is where visibility collides with conversion, because if there is no conversion, then visibility simply becomes a vanity metric (pro tip: you can't deposit those into your bank account). Not only is your brand being seen by the right audience, but now they are also buying what you are selling. Cha-Ching! Your actual strategy will be crafted and will drive the intentional development of tactics and campaigns to bring your vision to life. The Reach & Revenue phase is also powered by The Digital Day Planner, the content planner I developed during the pandemic.

When I spoke at conferences or conducted corporate training sessions, I would tell those in the room that the key to making digital marketing a success, and maintaining consistency in showing up for your followers online, is to create an editorial calendar and schedule your content. If your content is not planned, it essentially becomes a monkey on your back if you are having to constantly stop throughout your day to try to "get something posted" online. It occurred to me that while I was giving them great advice about making their digital content more manageable, there wasn't a tool out there to support connecting their strategic plan to the content campaigns that would bring them to life…so I created one.

The Digital Day Planner is all about creating content that connects and then converts to cash.

Reach & Revenue is the part of The C.O.R.E.™ Model where we zero in on monetization strategy, ensuring that the things you post online are directly connected to the goals and objectives for your business.

Key Components:

> Strategy
> Content That Connects
> Content That Converts to Cash
> Community Building
> Ethical AI

Execution

The Execution stage is essentially where the rubber meets the road. It is the culmination of everything you have created up until this point and ensures you aren't just throwing content into the void. You're setting good, solid goals. You're making data-driven decisions and reaping the rewards. Let's back up a bit and talk more about goals. When the conversation about goals comes up, George T. Doran's SMART goals are typically top of mind, but I think we can take it a little further. Don't get me wrong, I think SMART goals are great, and I even made them a part of The Digital Day Planner —but I know you can SCALE them to the next level.

The most overlooked part of the digital strategy is the systems needed to keep it moving like a well-oiled machine. Execution in The C.O.R.E.™ Model is about consistent, intentional implementation, and is the place where you no longer just set goals—you achieve them because you have a real system in place to make sure they become your reality.

Key Components:
> Goals That SCALE
>
> The STAGE System
>
> Live Events

Digital Marketing in the Real World

The C.O.R.E.™ Model is a growth system that was created to illuminate and expose your blind spots so that you can recalibrate your focus and turn your digital presence into a purpose-driven profit center. It is the bridge between your current momentum and the next-level sustainability you'll need to maintain something legacy-focused and purposeful. It shifts you from the laziness of being a reactive content creator (sorry if I stepped on your toes there), to an intentional, proactive strategy yielding machine. The C.O.R.E.™ Model forces your business to stand on solid ground before you stack the next six or seven figures on top of it. The C.O.R.E.™ Model is not just about scaling up—it's about scaling smart. With C.O.R.E., you step out of survival marketing and into sustainable, strategic growth.

What Makes the C.O.R.E.™ Model Different

Most frameworks—and your favorite Instagram gurus—focus on tactics: how to post, when to email, what funnel to build, what you can cut corners on using the latest AI tools. C.O.R.E.™ is different because it's not just a digital marketing playbook; it's a real business-building tool.

It doesn't matter if you're reeling in $100K or $1M—if your foundation isn't stable, your growth will feel harder than it has to, and you will feel like you are stuck in a rhythm of hustle and grind. The thing about "the grind" is this: what happens when you are driving a manual transmission vehicle and you start grinding those gears?

Things get bumpy, uncomfortable, and can cause serious damage-because if you are grinding, you are out of alignment. The transitions between gears (or levels in your business) don't have to be a bumpy road—it can happen much smoother once you come into alignment with how things should flow. The C.O.R.E.™ Model isn't about hacks or trends. It's about establishing a structure that allows you to scale with sanity, serve at a higher level, and reclaim your time without sacrificing your ambition. Sounds amazing, right?

The C.O.R.E.™ Model is the blueprint for:

- Founders and CEOs of service-based brands who are ready to scale without chaos
- High-achieving experts who've built a reputation but need real operational and marketing infrastructure.
- Visionary leaders who are tired of owning a job and are ready to create a business that thrives.

You can't build a high-performance brand on shallow strategy, disjointed or non-existent systems, and lazy execution.

You need a C.O.R.E. at the foundation of your efforts.

Clarity to align your message with the market.

Operations to hold the weight of your vision.

Reach & Revenue systems to scale your impact.

Execution rhythms to build momentum you can measure.

Clarity

Mindset Matters!

"Before you begin the "business" of any strategy, you must MIND your business first."

Tisha Holman

You've been focused on the money and didn't think digital marketing was important…but you are beginning to realize that you're leaving money on the table.

You may have thought   the first part of your digital marketing strategy would be something like writing a business plan, picking a snazzy color palette, designing a logo or maybe coming up with a catchy name for your business. Not quite. Those things are important, and will come in time, but the true foundation of your business begins with your mindset. I am going to start here because the truth of the matter is nothing else in this book will be of any benefit to you unless your head is in the game. Those six inches between your ears is the space that can make or break a business so I think it is worth spending some time here to ensure you have the right perspective on where you are in this very moment and the digital marketing strategy that has the potential to change your life and business forever.

The best playbooks don't start with how things will be accomplished— they start with a plan. And before you can begin planning, you've got to get your mind right.

There are two consistent mindset challenges that I encounter with most clients I serve: 1. They say things like "I am not a tech person." or "I hate posting online." or 2. They lack the confidence in themselves and their ability to show up online and outshine their competitors. The issue with 1 is while it may be true that you are not a tech savvy person and do not have a strong interest in prioritizing managing your digital presence, the fact is, and Nelson Mandela said it best, "It always seems impossible until it's done." Do not allow your fears of the unknown in the digital space to become a "culture killer" in your organization (even and especially if right now the organization is just you). Your thoughts and words have power, and they don't always just impact you. Get your mind right. Are you speaking life or are you speaking doom and gloom over your business and your online presence? Your thoughts and the words you say are paving the way for you. Can you draw any correlation between what you have been casually saying and thinking concerning your online presence and the outcomes you are experiencing?

Technology is evolving so quickly that a business owner no longer has the luxury of not being a "tech-person". If you want to have any longevity in today's business climate, you have got to become one and fast! And even still, as you embrace the place technology has in your business, it's ok to figure out how to integrate things in a way that still allows you to stay in your zone of genius. This is where the strategy, the tactics, and the systems enter the chat. Napoleon Hill shares in his book, Think and Grow Rich, "There are no limitations to the mind except those we acknowledge. Both poverty and riches are the offspring of thought."

The second mindset challenge is the culprit that is stifling the potential of so many talented people—imposter syndrome. So, what exactly is imposter syndrome anyway and what does it have to do with my digital marketing strategy? I'm glad you asked! Imposter Syndrome is the imaginary glass ceiling that keeps brilliant people from sharing their greatness with the world. I would even go as far to say that for most people, it is a glass ceiling held in place by a problem they didn't know they had. Now that definition comes from the Book of Tisha, so let's also explore a more classical definition. According to the National Library of Medicine, "imposter syndrome describes high-achieving individuals, who, despite their objective successes, fail to internalize their accomplishments and have persistent self-doubt and fear of being exposed as a fraud of imposter." That's pretty deep, isn't it? Here's the thing — if you are reading this book, you are likely a high-achiever who has already knocked some amazing accomplishments out of the park, you just need to embrace your greatness a little tighter, because, if you didn't realize it, there are people out there in the digital space who are waiting on you to show up confidently and solve a huge problem in their lives. The irony of imposter syndrome is that the ones who probably should have a bit of it—don't, and they show up confidently in their lack of expertise to rake in the dough online.

MINDSET, ALIGNMENT, AND CONFIDENCE IN YOUR GIFTS ARE THE BEGINNING OF THE STRATEGY

You must rest comfortably in the confidence that the gifts and talents you possess are uniquely yours. You are a called and capable disruptor. You have everything you need to be an impact maker. You are the change agent that your ideal client is looking for. And yes, you will vibe with your tribe; but they have to be able to find you first. Maybe I'm dating myself a bit here, but a popular hit from 90's R&B group En Vogue comes to mind, "Free your mind, and the rest will follow!" No more downplaying, no more second guessing, no more overthinking. This is when you will see the power of alignment with your mindset and your digital marketing. When you do this, your life and business will never be the same.

We talked about the "trust tree" earlier, right? Ok, it's story time. Allow me to be transparent for a moment.

I decided to invest my time and my money into an amazing business coach. I mean she is truly a rockstar at what she does! She loaded me up with all of the tools and moxy that I needed to do what I am trying to help you do. I revamped my entire business model and created a few programs for my clients that for sure would provide them with the transformational results they needed to soar high in the digital space…and then did nothing with them. Literally and absolutely NO-thing. I was standing in my own way, and as brilliant and qualified as I am, I was still afraid to win. I had a baaaad case of imposter syndrome, so I know how many of you feel. I have been there myself and I have the t-shirt to prove it. Thinking back on that season stops me in my tracks today. How could I for even one iota of a second have believed that the gifts God gave me weren't enough? Why would I question the fact that people were waiting on me to show up and help them make life and business better? The truth of the matter is: I was afraid. I was afraid that people wouldn't pay my new prices (because they were much, much higher), even though I KNEW what I had to offer them had tremendous, business catapulting, life-changing value. Glad those days are behind me!

And as if an acute case of imposter syndrome wasn't enough, I also had to contend with people whose opinions I once valued, strongly telling me that I sounded like a professor all the time and my personality just didn't show when I posted online. I guess that was their nice way of saying I was boring online Yikes! More than one person said it, so it had to be true, right? But what do you do with that type of "feedback" when that is who you are? To give you some additional context, I was the original Akilah and The Bee! — a kid spelling bee champ, early, advanced reader, and still today an eternal word nerd who achieved an almost perfect verbal SAT score. I naturally speak like a "professor", and I don't apologize for it. The crazy thing is I internalized what they said to me and wondered if I would be able to compete with those content creators, who as I think back on it, were really just entertaining folks with anecdotal knowledge and half-baked business acumen that at the end of the day wasn't going to help them build and scale their business to greater profitability. Whew! They didn't have the experience I had but what they did have is the chutzpah to show up online confidently engaging the very clients that needed my gifts to take them to the goal line. I had to really do a gut check! Ultimately, I will own the fact that I did need to find and uncover balance so that I could share my brand with the world. I wanted to do it without losing myself in the process and in a manner that I could comfortably sustain. Enough had become enough. Can you relate? Now that I am on the other side of this, I can tell you: there is no better feeling than being free of the captivity of what other people think about you.

I am my own success story. Through extending grace and lovingly embracing myself, I became dedicated to only working with who I am supposed to work with, and from there, THE GAME CHANGED! New clients and unexpected opportunities began showing up at my doorstep. I discovered alignment at the intersection of who I truly am and the freedom of embracing, then sharing, that self with the world. Alignment is the magic word here, friend. Once you align your mindset and focus on that which you are called to, you will vibe with your tribe and things will start to work in your favor.

I am speaking from experience. I recognize this is something many high-achieving business owners quietly struggle with but just remember: Imposter Syndrome is a state of mind, not a diagnosis and the fix is an inside job. If left unchecked, it can be the difference between you thriving in your gifts as you plan for your next money milestone or you are remaining stuck, stagnant, broke and unhappy because you aren't aligned with your purpose.

Here are a few things I ask my clients who are struggling with this. I invite you to challenge yourself and answer these questions for yourself. Remember, the truth will set you free. Radical honesty here is what will help you overcome this hurdle that is diluting the power and potency of your gifts and talents.

TIME OUT!

1. When you think about your successes or accomplishments, what feelings come up for you?

2. How do you talk about your achievements with others? Do you downplay them, deflect praise, or find it hard to accept compliments?

3. What would you say to someone else experiencing imposter syndrome about their skills and value? And how might that advice differ from the way you treat yourself?

4. Can you recall a recent situation where you felt like a fraud or that you weren't "qualified" for the task at hand? What triggered that feeling, and how did you respond?

5. If you were to honestly assess your qualifications, experience, and skill set without external validation, what truths would emerge about your own competence?

Market Research

"If your goal is to build a sustainable business, you cannot afford to take shortcuts. Do your homework."

~*Tisha Holman*

I am a strong proponent of a data-driven strategy because it helps you make informed decisions about the ways in which you approach the task at hand. With that being said, let's kick this chapter off with a few statistics.

According to a recent study by Forbes, 73% of small business owners aren't confident their current strategy is contributing to their business goals. Moreover, 31% of small business owners are likely to procrastinate or ignore determining what is working strategically for their marketing. And sadly, data collected from the United States Bureau of Labor Statistics reveals that a staggering 50% of small businesses fail in the first 5yrs.

Market research is our starting point, especially if you have yet to establish your online presence. If you have already established your online presence, this step would include a digital marketing audit as well. (We'll explore that in the next chapter.) Before you begin building the foundation for your strategy, you have to understand the lay of the land. In a world of ephemeral content and hashtags, traditional marketing fundamentals are often overlooked. Don't skip the basics. Market research must be conducted so that you can get a true, objective idea of whether or not the services you provide are in demand for your target audience. This is also a great opportunity to take inventory of who your "competitors" are and what they are doing in the digital space. I put competitors in quotation marks, and use the term very loosely because I do not really believe in competition. Yes, there are others out there who may offer the same services you provide, but the difference is, they do not have the unique set of gifts and talents you possess, and they aren't called to serve the people you are called to impact. They don't have the recipe for your secret sauce! That secret sauce thing can sound a little cliche, so let me bring it closer to home for you. Have you ever asked a friend for the recipe of a dish that is their specialty—the one that when it is on the table, you can't get enough of it? The dish is so good, you'll discretely loosen your belt buckle just so you can make room for another helping, but then when they share the recipe and you try it at home, something is missing! You followed the directions to the T, but it just doesn't taste as good as when your friend makes it. This is the same with you and the services you provide. The market may be "saturated", and a lot of people do the same thing that you do, could even copy what they see you do—but they can never do it the way you do it. That being said, it is still good business sense to have an awareness of what others in your industry are doing, only for the purpose of strategizing how you can become a disruptive competitor and then commence to blazing trails around them.

I'm going to explain the various types of market research you can leverage to gain valuable insights about your target client, and the market you plan to serve. Some or all of these may be a good fit for you; apply what makes sense for your brand. Once you have conducted this research and leveraged your findings as the foundation of your digital marketing strategy, realize this isn't a one-time exercise. It is still a good idea to tap into your audience periodically so you can fine-tune your tactics as things evolve in your industry. My suggestion is to make this a part of your annual strategic planning. A data-driven strategy is one of the things that is going to be your secret weapon and set you apart from others simply because many are just too lazy to be bothered as they would rather "jump in" and build the plane while they are flying it.

I am going to define each method of research, share its potential use in digital marketing, then provide a real-world example of its application. I want you to have the best possible outcomes in this step of The C.O.R.E.™ Model.

Primary Research

Primary Research is research that you conduct yourself and involves gathering data first-hand and directly from the source. This could also include gathering data from your existing clients.

Use in Digital Marketing - Because you collect the data directly, you can focus on your exact target audience and relevant questions. Digital marketers use primary research to uncover unique customer pain points, test reactions to a new product/service concept, or gather feedback on brand messaging. This direct feedback helps shape marketing campaigns and product offerings with confidence that they address the audience's actual preferences and concerns

Real-World Example - A consulting firm with a high-ticket coaching program might conduct one-on-one interviews with past clients to learn why they signed up, and which aspects of the service delivered the most value. Through these interviews (a form of primary research), the marketer gains deep insight into client motivations and most impact language to help shape their CopySignature™. The findings can then guide the firm's messaging on all its platforms, emphasizing the specific benefits and transformational outcomes that clients mentioned. Similarly, the firm could run an online survey for its email subscribers, asking which topics or pain points are most important to them. The survey results (first-hand data) would help the firm refine its content strategy and tailor its high-end offer to what the audience truly wants.

Secondary Research

Secondary Research is data that already exists such as academic studies and competitor research.

Use in Digital Marketing - Marketers typically start with secondary research to get a broad understanding of the market or to kick off the exploratory phase of audience research. It's a cost-effective way to discover trends, benchmark those "competitors", and validate assumptions before diving into time-consuming primary research. In a solid digital marketing strategy, secondary research might involve reviewing published consumer behavior reports, analyzing competitor case studies, or mining public data (like census demographics or social media statistics) to profile your target audience. These insights highlight opportunities and gaps—for example, spotting an underserved segment or emerging demand—that can shape your strategy. Secondary research is also useful for service-based businesses to gather evidence that can be used in marketing materials to build credibility.

Real-World Example - Imagine a luxury travel agency planning a new high-end tour package. The marketing strategist for the agency might perform secondary research by reading an industry report on post-pandemic travel trends and affluent consumer preferences. They could also analyze competitor websites and online reviews to see what wealthy travelers praise or complain about. Through the analysis of these super valuable insights, the strategist builds a clearer picture of the target audience's desires— for instance, a growing interest in eco-friendly travel or personalized experiences. This secondary research saves the agency time (the data is already available) and guides how to position the new premium service. Only after this groundwork will they conduct primary research (like a focus group or survey) for more specific questions, which means the secondary data helped refine what to ask and prevented redundant efforts.

Qualitative Research - Qualitative Research is an approach that gathers non-numerical, in-depth insights into audience attitudes, motivations, and behaviors.

Use in Digital Marketing - In a digital marketing strategy, qualitative research helps explain the "why" behind customer behaviors. It provides color and context that purely numerical data can miss. Marketers use qualitative insights to shape brand messaging, tone, and value propositions so they resonate emotionally with the target audience because as you'll discover in a later chapter, the best brands tug on people's emotions. For instance, through interviews or reading open-ended survey responses, a marketer might discover the language customers use to describe their problem ("I feel overwhelmed by managing my finances"). They can then mirror those exact phrases in their copy online. Qualitative research is especially useful for service businesses, where purchase decisions are often highly personal or trust-based and understanding concerns and perceptions is mission critical to close them. Techniques like buyer persona interviews, customer journey mapping, or analyzing reviews all fall under qualitative research and guide marketers in crafting empathetic, targeted campaigns.

Real-World Example - A company offering an elite career coaching service conducts in-depth interviews with a dozen clients who successfully landed executive jobs after using the service. In these hour-long interviews, clients share stories about their job search fears, their aspirations, and how the coaching helped. The marketer listens for emotional cues — e.g., clients might say they "felt stuck and lacked confidence" before coaching, but now "feel empowered to negotiate a higher salary." These qualitative findings empower the marketing team to highlight those transformative feelings in their messaging (e.g., "from stuck in your career to confidently landing your dream job"). The rich, descriptive feedback also uncovers objections (like initial skepticism about the price) that the marketer can proactively address on the website's FAQ or in a webinar. This way, qualitative research ensures the marketing strategy speaks directly to the audience's mindset and builds trust by showing understanding of their journey.

Quantitative Research - Quantitative Research is an approach that focuses on numeric data and statistics to measure audience characteristics and behaviors.

Use in Digital Marketing - It provides hard numbers that can justify decisions and track performance. Marketers rely on quantitative data to segment the market (e.g. what % of users fall into different age brackets), measure campaign results (conversion rates, ROI). It can be and is often combined with qualitative research to paint a bigger, more colorful picture: numbers show what is happening, while qualitative insights explain why.

Real-World Example - A SaaS company that sells an enterprise software subscription uses quantitative research to improve its marketing funnel. The marketing team analyzes web analytics and finds that 5% of website visitors request a demo (conversion rate), and the average time on the pricing page is 45 seconds. They also send out a structured survey to 500 prospects asking them to rank the importance of various software features on a 1–5 scale. The survey reveals, for example, that 80% of respondents rate "24/7 customer support" as very important, while only 30% care about an AI feature. Armed with these numbers, the team makes data-driven decisions: they prioritize highlighting the support benefit in ad copy (since the majority value it) and they set a key performance indicator (KPI) to increase the demo request rate by tweaking the website (perhaps by adding a clearer CTA, then measuring the change). Over time, they can statistically track if marketing changes lead to higher percentages in desired actions. This use of quantitative research ensures the strategy is grounded in measurable evidence of what the audience is doing and what they prioritize.

I know this one can feel like it's pulling you into the nerdy weeds with the numbers - but it is so important for you and making intentional strategic business moves.

Focus Groups - Focus Groups are group discussions in which a moderator leads a small group of participants in conversation to gather opinions on a product or concept.

Use in Digital Marketing - In a marketing strategy, focus groups are used to probe deeper into customer opinions and preferred language before launching something to the wider market. They can validate whether a value proposition or marketing message resonates with the target audience, and how people articulate their needs or concerns.

Real-World Example - A marketing agency is developing a new high-ticket premium "all-in-one" marketing service package aimed at small businesses. Before fully rolling it out, they organize a focus group with 8 small business owners who fit their ideal client profile. During the session, the moderator asks the group to react to the service description, the proposed pricing, and a sample marketing campaign included in the package. As the discussion unfolds, the agency's team observes that phrases like "I'm not sure if it's right for my industry" keep coming up – indicating a positioning issue – and one participant's comment about budget concerns sparks others to agree. On the positive side, they notice excitement when talking about the convenience of an all-in-one solution ("It's appealing not to have to juggle multiple vendors" says one business owner, and others nod in agreement). These insights are insight gold for the agency's strategy. They decide to adjust their marketing copy to clarify industry customization options (addressing the uncertainty expressed) and prepare a comparison chart to justify the cost with ROI figures (addressing budget concerns). So, at the end of the day, the focus group provided group-validated insights that the agency can now use to refine its CopySignature™ and marketing materials before the big launch, increasing the chances that the offer will hit the right notes with potential clients.

Surveys - A survey is a research tool (usually a structured questionnaire) used to collect data from a target audience in a systematic way. Surveys consist of a series of questions — which can be closed-ended (multiple choice, rating scales, yes/no) —for quantitative data, or open-ended for qualitative feedback.

Use in Digital Marketing - Surveys are invaluable for gathering feedback at scale. They allow marketers to tap into their customer base or target demographic and quickly collect a large volume of information.

Real-World Example - A boutique financial advisory firm offering an expensive wealth management program wants to improve its marketing messaging. They decide to survey both current clients and qualified prospects. Using an online survey, they ask questions like: "Which factor was most important in choosing our firm?", "Rank the following benefits in order of value to you," and an open-ended question, "What nearly prevented you from signing up for our program?" After sending it to their email list and getting approximately150 responses, the firm uncovers clear patterns. For instance, 60% of respondents might say "expertise and credentials" is the top factor in choosing the firm, whereas only 10% cite pricing as the top factor, indicating that their high price point is not as big a barrier as they feared. In the open-ended answers, a common theme appears: several prospects mention they "weren't sure if the service would be personalized enough." Armed with this knowledge, the marketing team can take intentional action. With the new information, they might emphasize the firm's expertise more prominently on the website and add testimonials or case studies as social proof to highlight their highly personalized approach. Thanks to the survey, the firm has quantitative evidence (percentages and rankings) to guide where to focus its messaging, as well as qualitative hints from comments to refine how they communicate their value – all of which helps in marketing a high-ticket service more effectively.

You're probably familiar with the types of market research I just mentioned but let me share a couple of lesser-known examples that can become key tools in your marketing toolbox.

Digital Ethnography - Digital Ethnography is the observation of people in their natural surroundings - online behaviors

Use in Digital Marketing - Tracking a set of participants as they use a service over a period of time. For example, participants could be asked to keep a video diary of their daily interactions with a fitness coaching app, or to upload photos of their workspace if the service relates to office productivity for one week. This yields real-world usage insights: you might literally see frustrations or moments of joy and delight as they happen, rather than relying on memory. Marketers also do ethnographic research by observing online discussions

Real-World Example - A company offering a premium meal-planning and diet coaching service wants to deeply understand how busy professionals manage their nutrition throughout the day so they can tailor their marketing and service delivery options to their ideal clients. They undertake a digital ethnography study with 10 participants who are within their target audience (e.g., working professionals who have shown interest in fitness coaching). Each participant is asked to use a special mobile app journal for two weeks to log their food decisions, take photos of their meals or snacks, and record short videos at certain times (like when they feel a craving or when they skip a meal). Researchers also get permission to observe a dedicated Slack community where these participants chat about their meal-planning struggles. Through this digital ethnography, the marketing team gains eye-opening insights. For instance, one finding might be that around 3 PM, many participants reach for an unhealthy snack because they are feeling stressed between meetings – something that could not fully be captured by a standard survey. Participants' photos show the kinds of convenient (but unhealthy) foods they grab, and their video diaries reveal phrases like "I just don't have the energy to cook in the evening." These real-life observations allow the company to adjust its marketing strategy: they create content specifically addressing the "3 PM slump," and highlight how their service provides quick, healthy options that save mental energy. This level understanding gained through digital ethnography will help them differentiate their high-ticket coaching service in the market and connect with their target audience.

SWOT + T Analysis - You're probably familiar with a SWOT analysis, but in case you're not, it's a framework that identifies the Strengths, Weaknesses, Opportunities, and Threats of a given situation. I like to add an additional T to that formula for Trends. A solid SWOT+T analysis allows you to leverage strengths, address weaknesses, capitalize on opportunities, mitigate threats, and explore current trends.

Rather than showing its use in digital marketing and then a real-world example as I did earlier, I'm going to share an example of a SWOT+T instead.

Client's SWOT Analysis for Digital Marketing (Coach in the personal development space)

Strengths:

- Well-defined personal brand: Strong reputation within their niche, providing high-value content on their blog and social media channels. This builds trust and draws in an audience.
- Email list with high open rates: Solid email list, and subscribers are highly engaged with tailored advice and tips.

- Client testimonials and case studies: Social proof and success stories add credibility.

Weaknesses:

- Low social media engagement on newer platforms: Significant presence on Instagram, their engagement is struggling on LinkedIn.
- Inconsistent posts: Struggles with maintaining a content calendar and often misses posting opportunities, which impacts brand visibility.
- Website UX/UI issues: The website is not mobile-friendly, causing potential leads to bounce before converting.

Opportunities:

- Growth of video content: The rising demand for video content on YouTube presents an opportunity to pivot and integrate more video marketing into the strategy.
- Strategic Partnerships: Collaborations or joint ventures with influencers can help expand their reach.
- Increase in demand for online learning: Online learning platforms offer an opportunity to create and sell digital courses or exclusive webinars.

Threats:

- Increasing competition in the personal development space: More coaches and consultants are entering the market, leading to greater competition for the same target audience. *This is just an example, y'all already know I don't see this as a threat!

- Ad fatigue: Facebook and Instagram ads have become saturated in the personal development niche, reducing the effectiveness of paid campaigns.

- New privacy laws affecting email marketing: New regulations that impact how they gather and use email data, forcing them to possibly rework lead-gen strategies.

Trends

- New features being added to social platforms: Leveraging updates and new platform features that will increase engagement and play nice with algorithms.

- #TrendsAndChallenges: Before jumping into the hashtag craze of the latest dance or challenge, evaluate whether or not it is a good fit for your brand identity and if it will resonate with your audience.

- Artificial Intelligence: Exploring how emerging technologies like artificial intelligence can improve your business operations and productivity.

Ok, friends! I know this chapter covered a lot, but these concepts are essential for building a strong foundation—not just for your digital marketing strategy, but for your overall business operations as well. As I stated at the beginning of this chapter, your mileage may vary—all of these may not apply to your business, but most apply to us all. Trust the process and remember I'm not just sharing theory; I'm giving you the playbook that has taken many small business owners to the top of their game.

The Digital Audit

"Building a digital marketing strategy without conducting an audit first, is essentially building an unprofitable ship without a sail."

~Tisha Holman

A s I mentioned in the previous chapter, doing market research is an ideal starting point, if you have an existing presence or not. The digital audit is for those of you that currently have an established online presence, whatever that looks like for you.

Before you can begin developing your digital marketing strategy, you need to do an honest, realistic evaluation of what you currently have in place. Although it may be highly probable that significant adjustments need to be made, there may be some elements of what you currently have in place that can still be implemented into the plans for the new strategy. The biggest inventory you are going to need to take is identifying whether or not the content you have in place aligns with the direction in which you are looking to take your brand. I've shared graphics, videos, and quotes in the past that I wouldn't post today—not because they lacked value, but because my brand and my identity as a digital marketing strategist and coach have evolved. Some content simply no longer fits, and that's perfectly fine. When I rebranded recently, I archived a lot of older content for exactly this reason.

Your audit could get tricky if you don't have your accounts set up correctly and data is not being tracked. It is very common for business owners to use personal social media accounts for their business because organic reach can be better than business pages but there are consequences to that. There are key features that are not available to personal pages, most importantly data and analytics. I'm going to be honest with you; it also impacts your credibility as a serious business. I would liken it to using a Gmail address for your business as opposed to using a private domain - mindyourbusiness@gmail.com vs. tisha@myb.digital. If you can't say "amen", just say "ouch".

I digress.

In some cases, an audit may reveal the need to rebrand. This can be difficult for many businesses because people often feel emotionally attached to their brand identity—which is natural—but it's also important to stay realistic if changes are necessary. The work ahead involves developing a strategy that positions your business for greater exposure, access, and growth, so it's worth making sure every part of your brand is primed for maximum impact with your audience.

All your digital platforms need to be included in the audit, because all of your digital platforms play a key role in your overall strategy. I am going to share the digital marketing audit checklist I use to evaluate the digital platforms for new clients.

Operational Documents

- Brand Style & Editorial Guide
- Brand CopySignature™ Sheet
- Digital Marketing Strategy
- Strategic & Tactical Plan
- Standard Operating Procedures
- Digital Marketing Policy
- Key Performance Indicator Document
- Crisis Management Plan
- Privacy & Security Policy
- Content Repository
- FAQs & Approved Responses Document
- Content Calendar
- Data & Analytics Performance Tracker/Leaderboard
- New Hire Onboarding Process
- Client Management Process Document

Website

- Content Management System
- Search Engine Optimization Tools
- Customer Relationship Manager Integration
- Lead Generation Strategy/Automation
- Photos with Proper Tags and ALT Attributes
- Mobile Responsive Design
- Consistent Typography & Color Scheme
- Strategic Content Hierarchy
- Privacy Policy - Return/Cancellation Policy - Terms & Conditions
- Great Usability - Strategic Navigation
- Blog Content - Keyword Optimized and Back Linked
- Compelling Content with a Clear Call to Action
- Data & Analytics/KPI Review
- Re-Targeting/Re-Marketing Strategy

Email

- Email Marketing Tool
- Customer Relationship Manager Integration
- Intentional Audience Segmentation
- Tags Associated with Campaigns
- A/B and Multi-Variate Testing Process
- Data & Analytics / KPI Review
- Send Time Optimization
- Personalization
- Browser & Mobile Responsiveness
- Catchy Subject Line & Clear Calls to Action
- Regular Email Blast Opt-In Campaign Sequence
- Lead Magnet Campaign Sequence
- Client Entry Campaign Sequence
- Regulatory Compliance
- Omni-Channel Integration

Social Media

- Code of Conduct / Social Media Policy
- Customer Relationship Manager Integration
- Social Media Scheduler
- Optimized Bio and Contact Details
- Consistent Page Handles
- Content Pillars that align with Company Goals
- Content Development Plan
- Content & Editorial Calendar / Hashtag Strategy
- FAQs - General / Campaign Specific
- Content Optimized for your Target Audience
- Content That Converts to Cash
- Community Building Plan
- Clear Calls to Action - Tangible & Intangible
- Data & Analytics / KPI Review
- Omni-Channel Integration

Text Messaging

- Text Message Marketing Tool
- Customer Relationship Manager Integration
- Intentional Audience Segmentation
- Personalization
- Send Time Optimization
- Clear Call to Action
- Budget / Cost Management Plan
- Content Workflows
- Live Event Lead Strategy
- Compliance with SMS Marketing/Governance Regulations
- Content That Converts to Cash
- Keyword / CRM Tag Strategy
- Data & Analytics / KPI Review

Podcast

- Podcast Distribution Channel(s)
- Customer Relationship Manager Integration
- Scalable Production Tools
- Clearly Defined Audience
- Episode Structure
- Scripts / CopySignature™ Document
- Consistent Publishing Schedule
- Content Calendar
- Guest Management Procedures
- PR / Podcast Swap Plan
- Cross Promotion Plan (Events, Merchandise Sales, etc.)
- Data & Analytics / KPI Review
- Omni-Channel Integration

Paid Media

- Ad Distribution Channel(s)
- Customer Relationship Manager Integration
- Budget / Bid Strategy
- Clear & Specific Advertising Goals
- Clear & Defined Target Audience
- Identify Relevant / Appropriate Platforms
- A/B - Multi-Variate Testing Procedure Document
- Ad Campaign Optimization Plan
- Clear Call to Action
- Hot Lead Magnet
- Compelling Copy and Visual Assets (Images / Video)
- Data & Analytics / KPI Review

Graphics and Videos

- Designed for Target Audience
- Aligned with Campaign Goals
- Clear Asset Naming Conventions
- Accurate use of Logos, Brand Colors & Typography
- Correct File Size for Platforms
- A/B - Multi-Variate Testing Procedure Document
- Establish a Design Budget
- Content Development Workflows
- Compelling Copy and Visual Assets
- Clear Call to Action
- Data & Analytics / KPI Review

Competitor Audit

This is only for research purposes. Your goal here is to identify 3-5 of your top competitors and look for opportunities to differentiate and stand out in your industry.

- Products & Services
- Marketing Tactics
- Pricing
- Positioning
- Customer Service Experience
- Customer Sentiment
- What are they doing that seems to be working well for them?
- What types of content and tactics are giving them high engagement and a following that continues to grow?

SWOT Analysis

Please realize that any failures you identify as you navigate this audit are nothing more than opportunities for growth and development. Before we close this chapter, I also want to call out a few small but mighty areas that also need your attention in this audit:

- Google yourself and your business. What do you see? What did you learn about your business?

- Call out where your messaging is unclear. Remember, confused minds don't make decisions.

- Document where processes and systems don't exist. Gaps in processes and systems create gaps in your profits.

Finding The Perfect M.A.T.C.H.™

"You'll start to experience unprecedented growth once you embody the fact that the services you provide, and the products you sell are not meant to reach everybody."

~*Tisha Holman*

When it comes to describing one's ideal client or target audience, the industry standard is that they are typically known as client avatars or personas. I take the concept of creating these avatars/personas deeper because it has always been important to me that my clients spend a lot of time developing them. These avatars/personas literally drive everything else that you'll do, say, write, post, share online and in the real world.

So, we are going to approach this differently than you have before, and it will be the thing that will escalate your success as a business owner overall—not just online. You will likely create two sets of your Perfect M.A.T.C.H.™, no more than three—beyond that, your messaging can get murky. You want to create an environment in which your products & services, target audience and messaging are airtight. That is how you remain impactful, profitable, and positioned to scale.

Out with client avatars and personas…in with finding The Perfect M.A.T.C.H.™ for your business.

M - Magnetized to your (CopySignature™) messaging
A - Aligned with your methodology/framework
T - Triggered by a real, urgent need
C - Craving transformation through expert guidance
H - Has the budget and the boldness to invest in themselves

Allow me to double-click on these and provide you with additional context. The best way I can elaborate here is to introduce you to a couple of The Perfect M.A.T.C.H.™ profiles for Mind Your Business:

The Scaling Strategist

Best fit for my program, The Digital Marketing Kickstart

- M: Magnetized to your (CopySignature™) messaging. Drawn to your clarity-first, no-fluff approach to marketing. Feels seen when reading your content.

- A: Aligned with your methodology/framework. Excited by frameworks and systems. Loves the idea of CopySignature™ and wants structure, not chaos.
- T: Triggered by a real, urgent need. Their business has plateaued and they're over the guessing game and ready for clear, structured growth.
- C: Craving transformation through expert guidance. Desperate to trade burnout for a system that works. They're craving a purpose-driven, profitable execution so they can scale.
- H: Has the budget and the boldness to invest in themselves. Already making 6 figures+ and looking to reinvest for growth with a sense of urgency and intentionality because they know time is literally money.

Primary Pain point: "I'm doing too much—and it's not working. I need a better way to grow."

The Retreat-Ready Rebuilder

Best fit for my small-group intensive, The Digital Marketing Makeover Retreat

- M: Magnetized to your (CopySignature™) messaging - Attracted to your luxury-level execution and visionary energy. Thinks, "This feels like the reset I've needed."
- A: Aligned with your methodology/framework. Tired of course clutter. Wants immersive support, not fluffy surface-level anecdotal business acumen.
- T: Triggered by a real, urgent need. Has experienced success before but their brand, messaging, and systems haven't kept up.

- C: Craving transformation through expert guidance. Yearning for a reconnection with their business, messaging, products, and purpose—with a plan to back it up.
- H: Has the budget and the boldness to invest in themselves. Ready to travel, invest, and make bold business decisions to re-align and relaunch.

Primary Pain point: "I've outgrown my old strategy and I want a quick, fresh start with hands-on guidance."

Hopefully these examples give you the inspiration you need to ideate on creating The Perfect M.A.T.C.H.™ for your brand.

The Perfect M.A.T.C.H.™ framework doesn't negate the traditional elements of the persona/avatar— it's meant to enhance it. So, as you answer the questions below, do so with all of the elements of The Perfect M.A.T.C.H.™ in mind. If your answer doesn't hit all of the criteria, that is your indication that you are not digging deep enough and additional thought is needed to more clearly identify your Perfect M.A.T.C.H.™. Take this exercise seriously - as I mentioned earlier, this drives the language of your brand identity on all platforms - online and in the real world.

Demographics - Who Are They?

Demographics help you define the age, location, profession and background of The Perfect M.A.T.C.H.™

- Age - Each age group has different motivations and spending habits
- Gender - How does their gender influence purchasing behavior?
- Income Level - What is their buying power and willingness to invest?
- Geographic location - Local? National? Global? Your CopySignature™ will come into play here

Psychographics - What Drives Them?

Demographics tell you who your client is, but psychographics tell you why they buy. Gaining an understanding of their motivations, pain points and values will be an invaluable tool for you in this process

- Values & Beliefs - What matters to them? Do they prioritize convenience, sustainability, prestige or affordability?
- Pain Points - What is the problem they struggle with that your business solves?
- Goals - What do they want to achieve, and how can your business help them reach that goal?

Firmographics - B2B Service Providers

What are the characteristics of the companies you want to work with? This helps you determine whether or not they are a good fit for the services you offer

- Industry - What industry do they work in? (coaching, finance, law, healthcare)
- Company Size - Are you targeting solopreneurs, small businesses, mid-sized companies - also, how do they self-identify in this area?
- Revenue bracket - What is their annual revenue?
- Decision-makers - Who makes the purchase decisions? (CEO, Director of Marketing, Operations Manager)
- Company culture & values - What do they value as an organization? Community impact, innovation, sustainability, diversity

Buying Behavior - How Do They Make Decisions?

- Understanding the root of how they make buying decisions helps you develop more impactful messaging

- What influences their ultimate decision to purchase? (Client testimonials, referrals, urgency)
- Where do they conduct their research before they buy? (Your website, Google, YouTube, LinkedIn, Better Business Bureau)
- What are some of the objections they might have? (investment, ROI questions, "The Trust Tree")

Online & Social Media Usage Habits

You have to place yourself where they are.

- What are their preferred social media platforms? (LinkedIn, YouTube, Instagram, Facebook)
- Content Consumption - Blog posts, webinars, video, podcasts, white papers?
- Level of engagement - Do they lurk in the shadows, or actively engage and share content?

Customer Journey

What is the pathway they take to discover your business and then enter your marketing funnel?

- How did they hear about you? (Ads, referrals, search engine, social media, speaking engagements)
- What led them to enter your ecosystem? (lead magnets, free webinar, live enrollment event, case studies, JV partnership)
- What will make them a repeat client? (Results, relationship, exclusive access, ROI)

You're almost there! The next step is to personify your Perfect M.A.T.C.H.™—envision them, find an image that brings them to life! This needs to be documented as a guide for writing your brand's core messages. I call it your CopySignature™ which you will learn more about in the next chapter. It also needs to be added to your new playbook so that you and your team can always refer to it in your day-to-day tasks and operations.

Building A Brand In Demand

"Your brand is not how you see yourself -it's how others experience you."

~Tisha Holman

O ne of the greatest misconceptions when it comes to building a brand is that there is a cheat code hidden somewhere that will unlock viral content that leads to millions of dollars and followers. The world has become used to seeing the explosive success of influencers online, but they don't recognize that it can take years to become an overnight success. The fact of the matter is, there is no shortcut to sustainable success. And being the serious entrepreneur or business owner I know you are, that's your goal. So, what is the formula for building a sustainable, scalable brand that's in demand?

You've got to show up!

You have to let the world know you exist, and you have to demonstrate that you (and the services you provide) are the BEST answer to the worst, most excruciatingly painful problem they are experiencing in life/business.

It's easy for me to share this with you now, but I haven't always practiced what I teach. Honestly, it's almost embarrassing that I'm a digital marketing strategist, and until recently you could have followed me online without even realizing it. I've advised some of your most beloved celebrities, and I've been a trusted deciding voice in the success of many of your favorite brands online. Yet, here I was, making the magic happen for everyone else and meanwhile back at the ranch, my own brand really wasn't clearly defined because I just hadn't stopped to do what I know it takes to win in the digital space. When this discussion came up, I would quote anecdotal cliches like "It's like the cobbler's kids have no shoes, you know?" or "I'm like your hair stylist who is always wearing a ponytail, but everyone who sits in my chair gets up looking fly!" Excuses, excuses, excuses.

The turning point for me was when people who I thought knew my work well kept referring to me as "The Social Media Lady". Now in all fairness to them, I get that my book, The Social Media Makeover is a big reason for that. I have a signature talk and highly requested workshop centered around that content, so the connection does make sense. But in all actuality, I am a digital marketing strategist whose expertise goes much wider and deeper than social media. How was I going to shift this narrative? I was living the consequences of not clearly defining my brand and showing up to share it boldly, and consistently in the world. They were defining me based upon what I was showing them, and that is nobody's fault but my own.

My online presence should serve as the rubric for my Perfect M.A.T.C.H.™ prospects—or at least be the place where they form an undeniable connection and recognize that I'm the one who can help them reach a level of online success they haven't been able to achieve on their own.

Your brand has an identity, similar to the way you identified your Perfect M.A.T.C.H.™, and it needs to be authentically you and curated exclusively for your audience. Now, authenticity can be such a tricky thing and I see so many struggling with it online. But if this is just about showing up as your true self, why would this be so difficult for so many small business owners trying to grow their brand in the digital space? Social media has made authenticity weird—at least it did for me. Allow me to explain why.

What I'm about to say might make some of you uncomfortable—so be it. Somewhere along the way, 'authenticity' got twisted. It became best-selling business books with the F-bomb in the title, going live in a messy house looking like you're overdue for a bath, or crying on camera about personal struggles. On the flip side, it also became going live at 6 a.m. with flawless makeup and perfect hair, as if that's the daily norm. None of that is me. None of that fits my brand. Yet I watched it work for so many others—in my industry and beyond—and I caught myself asking, should I show up like that too? My hang-up was my audience. Because my programs fall into the high-ticket category, I worried that what was being labeled as 'authentic' might actually misalign my brand with their needs. That left me stuck in a real conundrum.

I encourage you to challenge notions of what authenticity truly means and define it for yourself. You don't have to dance to trending audio clips on social media platforms to build. Don't just be authentic, be authentically disruptive and take up space in your industry as the thought leader and expert that you are. Whatever authenticity looks like for you, make sure it's a space that you are comfortable in so it's sustainable.

The Visible Leader

There are two sides to this branding coin: Defining who THEY are and figuring out who YOU are.

You are the CEO of your business, and CEOs can't hide in the corner office on the top floor anymore. Your personal brand is inextricably connected to the brand you are building, and your audience online expects for you to be a visible leader. People want to know who you are, and they want to know your "why". As if building your digital strategy and all that entails were not enough, you've also got to be sure you are positioning yourself as the expert and thought leader who is qualified to be an authority in the space you occupy!

Being on the visionary side of trends in your industry is going to be one of the things that will go a long way towards establishing thought-leadership online.

Story time.

I am an unsung visionary in the digital space—and that's on me. It's a huge disappointment to realize that if I had stayed consistent and positioned myself as the expert and thought leader I truly am, I'd likely be recognized among the top voices in my field. I was ahead of my time in several areas, but I dropped the ball when I should have kept running toward the end zone.

The first instance was the development of a mobile app. When apps first hit the scene, I was still an event planner. I planned beautiful social events and weddings, as well corporate events and conferences. I have always naturally sought to identify what others in my space were not doing so I could differentiate myself in the market. I can say that at the time, this was something ahead of its time that nobody else was doing in the events space, but of course it is very common today. I designed and developed a mobile app that my client's guests could download and RSVP to their events. You could get all of the event details, make your meal selections, share dietary restrictions and food allergies, access the gift registry—all of the things! You might be thinking this isn't such a big deal, but again, the concept was ahead of its time.

Here is the big one: the podcast. About seven years ago, I started a podcast when they were jussst starting to catch on. I interviewed founders of platforms like Hootsuite and Co-Schedule and other leadership and key players in organizations that anyone would be hard-pressed to gain access to today without a huge, monetized following. My home-grown studio wasn't anything fancy and during those days it didn't really need to be. I recorded my episodes with an unreliable wi-fi connection on Zoom and edited them in Garage Band with my limited knowledge of anything related to quality sound. I really can't say what made me stop recording and not even release some of the episodes. Maybe it was the fact that podcasts were still new, and engagement was kind of scarce, so I tapped out thinking it was just a flash in the pan.

Or maybe it was my own insecurity about the production quality, so I allowed imposter syndrome to get the best of me. Or maybe, (probably), it was a combination of the two. In either case, I shouldn't have given up. Had I stayed in the game, who knows what the podcast could have grown to be; the conversations were great and the topics being discussed were solid.

The point of sharing these stories is to reiterate the fact that sharing your expertise, establishing yourself as a thought leader, and trusting your intuition as a visionary are sometimes a very long, uncertain game but you and I both know that's what achieving real success as a business owner can oftentimes be. Stay the course my friend and keep building a brand that is in demand. There is no such thing as an oversight success.

What Is Your Story?

So, we have talked about your brand and what building intentionally means, but what about your story? Everyone doesn't have a hard-knock life, rags to riches story, but everyone should have a compelling 'why" for what they are doing. Tell your real story, one that you are comfortable sharing, and show your audience that you are the qualified one to guide them to and through the next phase of business.

I remember attending a brunch and the keynote speaker, a founder of a major brand, began to tell the audience about her upbringing and journey to entrepreneurship. When the speaker mentioned that she was from my hometown, my ears perked up. I am from Sacramento, California and I don't encounter people from the city often, so I was excited to make the connection. As I sat at my table, it was so awesome to be able to identify with some of the references that were being made but then things went left. In an effort to create a dramatic "rags to riches" story, she started to describe the city in a way that was just categorically false. She made it sound as if Sacramento was the lovechild of all the toughest hoods in the nation.

That simply is unnecessary. Your authentic story does not need to be curated fiction. You showing up as who you are is enough, and you will vibe with your tribe.

Digital Storytelling

Digital Storytelling is something that you need to become very adept at as you refine and strengthen your brand identity. It matters not only online, but also in person—whether at speaking engagements, in media appearances, or other settings. The strongest brands are the ones that connect emotionally. As a part of the discovery of who your Perfect M.A.T.C.H.™ is, you learned a lot about what is bothering them in life and business, and in the next chapter you'll discover how to curate magnetic messaging that triggers them to buy. Your job is to make all these elements do an intricate dance along with great storytelling to create a brand that is literally irresistible.

When you are talking to your target audience online, use your "inside" voice. I know you are thinking, "Ok, Tisha, what do you mean by that?" I am so glad you asked. A huge way that your storytelling and messaging will stand out online is to always make it about your audience. It is easy to fall into the trap of posting the content and talking about the things that you think are most relevant and will bring in the most sales. Don't be that person. Make everything about your target audience by speaking directly to their needs, not what feeds your ego. While you are at it, you'll have a much stronger impact if you create a "contrarian" narrative— put them in the story loop and close it with the solution you offer. Let me give you a few copy hook examples that demonstrate what I mean by "contrarian".

⇒ The one thing you are missing that is keeping you broke instead of booked and busy.

⇒ The 3 things nobody tells you about success online that everybody needs to know.

⇒ Here is the reason you aren't making any sales online.

The Psychology of Color

I often stress that your brand is way more than a snazzy color scheme. There are psychological elements of color that you should consider as you choose the colors for your brand or re-brand. German politician, poet, and artist Johann Woolfgang von Goethe is credited with the earliest exploration into the phenomenon of color in his book Theory of Colours that was published in 1810. Although his assertions were largely intuitive, he was definitely on to something. Years later, psychiatrist Carl Jung expanded on the psychology of color, suggesting that we all share a universal emotional response to it—so yes, my friends, this is something real that you should factor in as you build your brand. I know you may have some colors that are your favorites, but they may not be the ones that evoke the desired, subconscious response from your target audience. Take a look!

COLOR PSYCHOLOGY

Red	Bold, Courageous, Energetic	CNN, Netflix, Coca-Cola, Adobe
Orange	Friendly, Cheerful, Fun	The Home Depot, Nickelodeon, Popeyes
Yellow	Happiness, warmth, positivity	McDonalds, Ferrari, Nikon
Green	Balance, Health, Growth	Starbucks, Whole Foods, Spotify
Blue	Trustworthy, Dependable, Intelligence	HP, Samsung, PayPal
Purple	Wise, Nobility, Wealth	Taco Bell, Hallmark, Yahoo
Pink	Sensuality, Hope, Happiness	T-Mobile, Barbie, Lyft
Brown	Reliable, Stable, Honest	UPS, M&Ms, Hershey
Black	Power, Prestige, Classic	Uber, Sony, Prada
Gray	Professional, Calm, Stable	Apple, Mercedes-Benz, Nintendo
White	Purity, Innocence, Clarity	Nike, MAC, Sony

Now, of course, these are just examples and open for interpretation, but just keep it in mind for how you want your brand to be perceived online and in the real world.

With this in mind, are you ready to Get B.R.A.N.D.E.D.™?

The 7 Pillars of a Brand in Demand™ - Get B.R.A.N.D.E.D.™

This isn't just about having a logo and a color palette. It's about building a brand presence so clear, so magnetic, and so masterfully positioned that your ideal clients seek you out, refer you before they've even worked with you, and pay you without hesitation. The goal is to create a client culture that prioritizes the intangibles, because the strongest brands pull on emotion. And as I mentioned earlier, acronyms are part of what makes this playbook stick—so let's Get B.R.A.N.D.E.D.™!

B - Bold Belief & Brand Vision (Inspiration) The why behind your brand—your conviction, your cause.

- What are you here to change, challenge, or lead in your industry?

This is the heart and soul of your brand - your mission, beliefs, and your "why now?" message

R - Relevance & Revenue Positioning (Positioning)

This is where the market research we discussed earlier enters the chat.

- Do they need what you are selling?
- Are you solving a problem they even care about?

Take up space in your industry and align with what your ideal clients are actively searching for and willing to pay for. This is your transformational promise. Your category, your promise, and your pricing power.

A - Authentic Differentiation (Differentiation)

- What makes you unforgettable?
- What do you want to be known for?

This is your unfair advantage. This includes your story, your results, and where you identify your competitive edge and develop the recipe for that secret sauce we talked about earlier that your competitors couldn't duplicate if they tried.

N - Nail the Experience (Systems + Operations)

From your offer to delivery to client retention—this is how your brand is experienced and felt. The greatest brands are emotional, remember? Client journey, brand touchpoints, and operational excellence, irresistible offers.

D - Data-Driven Strategy (Strategy + Audit)

Make intentional moves by measuring what matters most. Social media content, website traffic, and your email campaigns. All powered by facts not feelings— data driven, targeted and intentional.

E - Elevated Identity (Visual & Verbal Brand)

The way your brand looks, sounds, and shows up online. These are your brand's style and editorial guides. Visuals, voice, tone, and content style that reinforces your CopySignature™.

D - Digital Storytelling (Brand Personality + CopySignature™)

This is the part that sells and converts your content to cash. Your brand voice, signature phrases, and value-driven storytelling that converts. What is your story? Your "authenticity" doesn't have to meet the hard-knock life examples we see a lot online. You, just the way you are, will be enough to vibe with your tribe.

Elements of the Brand Guide

- Mission/Vision statements
- Company core values
- Perfect M.A.T.C.H.™ descriptions
- Your CopySignature™
- Color palette - (RGB, CMYK, HEX)
- Typography
- Approved images
- Content pillars
- Editorial style guide
    - Your CopySignature™
    - Slogans and taglines
    - PC phrasing i.e.: Midget/little person

Creating Your CopySignature™

**"It's not that you aren't showing up
- it's that you're showing up forgettable...and
forgettable doesn't get funded."**

~Tisha Holman

CopySignature™ is your signature messaging system that positions you to communicate with clarity, convert with confidence, and stand out online. CopySignature™ is the tool that brings clarity to how you, and others, talk about your brand. It becomes language that not only converts, but it sounds like YOU across all of your platforms—exuding confidence in every conversation, caption and campaign. It is more than just swipe content for cute social media captions, and this isn't just something for personal brands - it's for serious small businesses that want to make an indelible imprint on their audience.

Is that you? If so, keep reading, it gets better!

Your CopySignature™ is made up of five pillars that carry the key messages your brand needs as you build your strategy. Think of it as the soul of your brand—the unique way your messaging resonates with your audience and calls them to act. And here's the proof: when people start quoting you, you'll know it's working.

5 Pillars

Power Pitching - Elevator pitch - clear, concise and magnetic (bios, intros, interviews)

- Who you are
- Who you help
- What you help them do/achieve/accomplish
- Why it matters

Let's Be Clear - Define your three key message pillars. These are the consistent throughlines your audience should always associate with your brand. (Content, web copy, webinars, conversation)

- Your unique value proposition
- Your transformation promise
- Your positioning hook

The Value - Infuse your brand voice and tone into your copy so your audience feels you when they read your words. (sales pages, email marketing, captions)

- What you sound like (voice)
- How you show up (tone)
- Emotional triggers you leverage (language + energy)

Signature Soundbites - Build a go-to bank of repeatable phrases, slogans, taglines, and power statements. (launches, branding, digital storytelling)

- Your high-impact one liners
- Your brand promise statement - 10 words or less
- Call to action phrases that feel like YOU

The Message Map - Create a message matrix for where and how your CopySignature™ lives across your brand. (marketing strategy, team training, brand audits)

- How to show up on each platform
- What language or tone adjustments
- Where your message leads (funnel into your ecosystems + CTA flow)
- FAQ/Monitoring documents - General, Campaign specific, Live events

The Power of the CopySignature™

A CopySignature™ does three mission critical things for your business in the digital space and in the real world:

1. Magnetizes the Right People: It speaks directly to your Perfect M.A.T.C.H.™ audience and magnetizes them to your messaging.

2. Establishes Market Authority: Your message positions you as the go-to expert, solidifying thought leadership and positioning you as the best answer to the problem they have in life and business.

3. Drives Conversions with Less Effort: It puts you and your messaging into alignment, making everything flow faster so you see steady profits and exponential growth.

Contrary to Popular Belief

Remember that contrarian messaging we just talked about? Well, here it is again. Your CopySignature™ must reflect a point of view that interrupts the norm. It's not just about what you say—it's about what you stand against, what you reframe, and what you challenge (contrarian). You become the voice that represents a transformation no one else in your industry is offering and it therefore makes you the clear choice. You have to make them uncomfortable with the current state of their life and business by hitting them where it hurts so those emotional triggers are pulled…then provide them with the pain relief.

Signature Phrases & Repeatables

Think about Starbucks. You don't go there and order a medium iced coffee—you get a grande cold brew because there is a language they have cultivated that is the fabric of who they are and has created community. Think about catch phrases you hear that lead you to immediately recognize a brand.

Messaging Anchors

Every CopySignature™ includes messaging anchors—themes you return to again and again. These themes help you organize your brand story, nurture sequence, offers, and thought leadership.

How to Develop Yours

Here's how we typically guide clients through the process inside The Digital Marketing Kickstart or during The Digital Marketing Makeover Retreat intensive:

1. Discover – Identify your client's language, core beliefs, and the pain points that are the greatest opportunities for transformation.

2. Frame – Identify your "voice", signature phrases, and repeatables.

3. Refine – Test your content (email, social, ads, etc.) and adjust based on what the data tells you— remember you are powered by a data-driven strategy

4. Document – Add it to the operational documents for you, your team, and your copywriters.

5. Go Live! – Incorporate it into content strategy, sales pages, launches, and onboarding workflows.

TIME OUT!

I want you to take a moment to reflect on a few things that may be very helpful as you develop your CopySignature™. You are establishing the lexicon for your brand, and I want you to look at this from all possible angles.

Take a few moments and thoughtfully answer the questions below:

What 3–5 bold beliefs do you hold about your industry, your work, or what it takes to succeed?

If your brand walked into a room, how would it speak? What phrases, energy, or cadences would it never use? This will be helpful as you develop your editorial calendar.

What phrases do you repeat on sales calls, in DMs, or in your client sessions? That's your gold.

What are 3 things you disagree with in your industry that your ideal client still believes?

What are 3–5 recurring ideas that underpin everything you teach, say, or sell?

Leading Execution at an Executive Level

"Executives who build visibility inside their organization build opportunity outside of it."

~Tisha Holman

Most professionals approach digital strategy as a collection of tasks: content, campaigns, timelines, analytics, and production. These elements matter, but they are only one dimension of execution. The executive layer lives above the tactical. It is where leadership, communication, psychology, and long-term positioning begin to shape how others perceive your value and expertise.

In this chapter, we step into that layer. The level where execution becomes a leadership behavior—not simply a marketing activity. The level where your digital presence becomes a strategic asset that amplifies your influence, expands your opportunities, and reflects the depth of your thinking.

Executives—whether in corporate environments, nonprofit leadership, or entrepreneurial ecosystems—now operate in a world where visibility is part of performance. The leaders who show up with clarity and authority online are the ones who shape conversations, attract partnerships, inspire trust, and ultimately position themselves for advancement.

Why Executives Must Manage Their Digital Footprint with Intention

The landscape has shifted. Influence is no longer determined solely by résumés, job titles, or years of experience. Increasingly, it is shaped by how you articulate your expertise, how you participate in industry conversations, and how confidently you demonstrate your point of view.

Executives with a strategic digital presence benefit in several ways:

- Their ideas travel farther, and their insights reach people beyond their immediate circle.

- Their leadership philosophy becomes clear, consistent, and memorable

- Their visibility positions them for speaking engagements, board appointments, advisory roles, and internal advancement.

- Their expertise becomes easier to recognize, validate, and refer.

Conversely, executives who remain invisible online unintentionally allow others to define the narrative. They risk being labeled as disengaged, behind the curve, or disconnected from the pace of modern communication. In corporate environments—where thought leadership, communication skills, and strategic clarity are now measured indicators of leadership readiness—silence can be costly.

You need a digital strategy not because you want attention, but because your expertise needs to flourish in both reach and influence.

Elevating From Participant to Architect

Architecting your digital strategy requires stepping back to examine the bigger picture:

- What do you want your leadership to be known for?

- How should your voice influence your industry?

- What does your digital footprint communicate about your depth, standards, and expertise?

- How should opportunities find you?

Your digital presence is an existential part of your brand and reflection of your professional approach to transformational leadership. This is what I refer to as executive identity alignment—the intentional connection between your leadership identity and your digital strategy. When they reinforce one another, your presence becomes a catalyst for career advancement, legacy, and influence.

The Three Layers of Executive-Level Strategy

For executives, your digital presence must reflect three core dimensions. These dimensions work together to communicate your leadership value and strategic intelligence.

1. Executive Voice

Your executive voice is the articulation of your expertise, values, philosophy, and perspective. It should communicate depth and your ability to interpret information, identify patterns, and make sense of complex issues.

An effective executive voice is:

- Clear: your ideas are easy to follow.
- Distinct: your perspective carries your signature.
- Consistent: your message aligns with your leadership values.
- Insightful: you contribute meaningfully, not performatively.

This is where your CopySignature™ principles naturally apply—not in explicit application, but in the way your message carries recognizable clarity and authority.

Executives with a strong voice online quickly become reference points in their industry. Their perspectives set the tone for how others think about emerging trends, organizational challenges, and strategic direction.

2. Executive Visibility

Visibility at the executive level is not about frequency and should reinforce who you are as a leader.

This includes:

- Thoughtfully crafted posts on platforms such as LinkedIn
- Articles or insights that provide perspective on industry issues
- Participation in panels, webinars, and conferences
- Sharing your leadership journey and professional development

Visibility creates familiarity, familiarity builds trust, and trust accelerates opportunity.

3. Executive Value

Your digital presence should clearly communicate the value you bring to the table—not through self-promotion, but rather through thoughtful demonstration.

This includes:

- Showcasing accomplishments with context and insight
- Sharing lessons learned from your leadership experiences
- Articulating what you believe drives impact and results

This is not a suggestion that you build an online presence focused on proving yourself. It's about creating transparency around the principles and approaches that define your leadership and contributions to your industry.

Building a Brand Inside a Corporate Environment

Executives often ask: "How do I build my personal brand without overstepping my organization?" The truth is, the two can coexist harmoniously when approached with intentionality.

A strong personal brand does not threaten your organization; it strengthens it. When people are clear about the type of leader you are, your organization benefits from the increased credibility, visibility, and trust you bring to your role.

To build your brand while honoring your corporate environment:

- Align your message with your core expertise rather than proprietary information.
- Use your presence to spotlight themes your organization values.
- Share your leadership philosophy and lessons learned without breaching confidentiality.
- Offer commentary that elevates the profession, industry, or discipline.

Executing at the Executive Layer

Executing at this level requires intentional planning and consistent application. Here is a concise roadmap to follow:

1. Define your leadership narrative. Identify what you want to be known for, who you serve, and what impact you want to have.
2. Develop a thought-leadership platform. Determine where and how you will share your expertise
3. Establish a visibility rhythm. Choose a sustainable cadence for posting, writing, or engaging.
4. Integrate your expertise into your digital footprint. Use stories, insights, and leadership reflections to build trust.
5. Expand your influence. Participate in speaking engagements, panels, media opportunities, or organizational initiatives.

Your digital presence is part of your professional legacy. When executed at an executive level, it becomes a strategic asset that supports your career trajectory, your influence, and your ability to lead with authority.

Section Summary: Clarity

Action Tasks

1. Define Your Brand's North Star: Write a single, definitive statement that captures who you serve, what you deliver, and why it matters.

2. Eliminate Messaging Fluff: Identify 3 phrases you've been using in your marketing that are vague or cliché. Rewrite them into sharp, specific statements.

3. Audit All Copy Assets: Review website, sales pages, and social bios. Highlight anything that doesn't instantly communicate value or differentiation.

Prompts

If your dream client read your bio right now, would they immediately know why you're the best option?

What specific words or phrases make your ideal audience feel seen and understood?

Where are you overcomplicating your message in an attempt to sound "professional" or "big"?

Exercises

Magnetic Message Drill:

Fill in this template, then refine it until it feels powerful:

"I help [WHO] achieve [OUTCOME] through [METHOD], so they can [BIGGER IMPACT]."

Copy Relevance Test:

Have 3 people in your ideal audience read your core offer description. Ask

1. What did you hear?
2. What stood out?
3. What was unclear?

Rewrite the offer description based on their feedback.

Operations

The Operations component of the C.O.R.E.™ Model is the most underestimated pillar of long-term scalability. While marketing and branding often get the spotlight, it's your internal systems—the invisible engine behind your client experience, service delivery, and overall business rhythm—that determine the true trajectory of the growth of your organization. Now you may be wondering, "What do my business systems, policies, and procedures have to do with my digital marketing strategy?" EVERYTHING! If these areas of your business are not hitting on all cylinders, it will also impact your marketing strategy. What happens when you mix rotten fruit with fresh fruit? The rotten fruit spreads to the fresh fruit and kills it too. This is the same for your business—and it is also why I am not your average digital marketing strategist. Together, we are going to build something that elevates your business in its entirety.

Strong operations —or, should I say, the lack thereof —is the silent killer of momentum in high-achieving service businesses. You can have magnetic messaging, an irresistible offer, and a growing audience, but if your backend is a mess, you are, as some of our more seasoned folks used to say, "cutting your nose off to spite your face." Broken workflows and undocumented processes are very costly in terms of time, money, energy, and your ability to scale. It's just not worth the frustration they bring to you and your team. In this phase of the C.O.R.E.™ Model, we are documenting policies, procedures, and systems—implementation and execution will come later.

Are you familiar with the term operational drag? Operational drag refers to any disorganization or inefficiencies that impede processes, profits, or productivity. Are you experiencing any of these bottlenecks that lead to operational drag?

- Your team is often confused or constantly asking for clarity.
- You secretly dread client onboarding because it's always a bumpy road.
- You feel like things are always "on fire," even when revenue and growth seem to be good.
- Your tech tools don't talk to each other, and tasks fall through the cracks.
- You can't trust the business to run—or it literally can't—without your real-time input and presence...THIS one is the kicker!

If any one of these culprits of operational drag applies to you, this phase of the C.O.R.E.™ Model will be the relief in your business you did not realize you desperately needed!

Let's get started!

The 5 Operational Layers of a Scalable Service Business

In the C.O.R.E.™ Model, Operations isn't a single system. It's an intricately layered stack that becomes the infrastructure that works together to support your business's most critical functions.

Let's break each one down.

CEO Command Center

Clarity in your business's operational aspects starts at the top. As the CEO, you are the visionary, setting the tone and rhythm of the business. This is your control panel. It's what allows you to zoom out and see the business from a vantage point that keeps you in your lane as a leader who works ON the business, not IN the business. Without the awareness of this data and information, you're flying blind and probably very frustrated.

This centralized command center or dashboard gives visibility to:

- **Annual, Quarterly, and Monthly Goals** - Goals yield the discipline you need to stay productive
- **Key Performance Indicators** - What doesn't get measured in your business doesn't get done.
- **Core Projects & Events by Quarter** - You have to be able to plan and track where the money is coming from
- **Launch & Event Timelines** - This is critical for campaign development and editorial calendar planning.
- **Team Capacity Planning** - You have to know who is going to get the work done.
- **Client Pipeline Lifecycle Status** - This supports intentionality around lead generation and monitoring their progress through your client lifecycle.
- **Lead Tracking** - Where do your hottest leads come from? Where is your pot of gold for the highest converting leads?

There's a System for That

"Systems are the difference between running your business and your business running you."

~*Tisha Holman*

Having strong documented systems, policies, and processes allows your business to deliver a consistent, elevated experience no matter who's buying or who's facilitating. The way you deliver your services is just as important as how you sell them.

For every core offer, you'll need:

- A clear onboarding process (marketing automations and materials that create a keen understanding of what your new client can expect working with you and your team.)
- A documented client journey (what happens at every touchpoint and milestone of their time with you?)

- Internal Standard Operating Procedures for your team (delivery checklists, handoffs, quality checks, 3rd party vendors, documentation, client engagement, and more!)
- Offboarding workflows (testimonials, referrals, renewals, surveys)

Roles, Rhythms, and Results

A high-functioning team doesn't just "get stuff done" on its own. They become a well-oiled machine with a strong rhythmic flow when roles and expectations are clear, ownership of duties & tasks is defined, success is measured, and progress is evaluated.

This layer includes:

- Role Clarity & Scorecards: Every person has measurable outcomes tied to their productivity, not just a task list.
- Weekly Rhythm: Team meetings, syncs with leadership, and other ancillary updates.
- Project Management software that reflects the real-time status of all work-in-progress.
- Content Repository: A centralized hub for SOPs, processes, and team trainings that eliminate siloes of document ownership.

Tech Tools That Talk

One of the fastest ways to lose time, data, and momentum is with a fragmented tech stack. If your email marketing tool, CRM, calendar, payment processor, and project management tools are all siloed, you're not running a business; you're likely juggling one —and I would venture to guess not very well. To keep this conversation as evergreen as possible, I won't make specific tool suggestions, but I will share what you should be including. The bottom line is automation, well-structured sequences, and strong feedback loops in all the possible places.

Your operational tech stack should cover:
- Lead capture > CRM tagging
- Client onboarding > Email workflows and automations
- Scheduling > Time zone logic buffers
- Task tracking & project management
- Data dashboards for performance visibility

Scalable Infrastructure

This part will feel very tedious and labor-intensive on the front end, but the long-term payoff is priceless and will be the difference between a business that needs you and a business that runs with you. Once all these things are locked in, it will be the wing beneath your wings when you are ready to hire staff and expand the services you offer.

Your scalable infrastructure includes:
- Standard Operating Procedures Library: Documented step-by-step processes for ALL recurring tasks

- A key asset vault that is a central location for approved headshots, bios, course descriptions, workshop/keynote session details, slide decks, swipe copy, videos, and templates...EVERYTHING!

- Financial Operations: Accounts payable and accounts receivable processes, periodic financial reporting guidelines to keep you dialed in to the money flowing through your company.

- Operational KPIs: You'll have to determine how you'll measure success in your organization—internally (business ops and your digital marketing) and externally. Whatever it means for you, put it in writing.

Reclaiming Your Time

Leveling up your company to operational excellence isn't about micromanaging your team; it is about empowering them to support your growth and success. The goal is to make space for freedom, laced with structure, that allows you to be more innovative and creative while reclaiming your time so you can focus on the areas of your business that rake in the big bucks.

What You're Actually Building: Your Operational Core

Let's zoom back out and look at the "what" and the "whys" of this phase of the C.O.R.E.™ Model:

Operational Element	What It Does	Why It Matters
CEO Command Center	Sets priorities, plans initiatives, and tracks KPIs	You make data-backed decisions and lead proactively
There's a System for That	Ensures consistent client results	Builds your brand reputation + increases referrals
Roles, Rhythm, and Results	Clarifies who owns what and how	Minimizes confusion, micromanagement, and burnout
Tech Tools that Talk	Automates and connects systems	Reduces time waste and operational errors
Scalable Infrastructure	Codifies business processes for repeatability	Enables delegation, growth, and higher margins

TIME OUT!

Identify the three most inconsistent or disjointed areas in your backend right now. Then, begin to work through developing documentation and policies that will resolve the inconsistencies and streamline the tasks for your team.

Operational Documents

**"Be proactive, not reactive
when it comes to laying the operational
foundation for your business."**

~Tisha Holman

B elow you will find a list of the operational documents that you should have in place for your business. Everyone who joins your organization should have access to the documentation for all policies, procedures, and systems. I know it has been a while, but do you recall, earlier in the playbook, I talked about McDonald's and how all of their store managers are trained at Hamburger University, the global center for operations and training development? Everyone who works at McDonald's is doing everything the same way, which is why the Big Mac© and the other accompanying menu items taste the same no matter what location you go to—your company shouldn't be any different.

Every new addition to your team should be trained to do things your way because you have taken the time to identify what is most efficacious (I really love that word) for your internal operations and how your clients are served.

Mission/Vision Statement

Core Values

Organizational Chart

CopySignature™

Perfect M.A.T.C.H.™

Brand Style Guide

Editorial Guide

Standard Operating Procedures

Key Performance Indicators

Social Media Conduct Policy

Crisis Management Policy

Credential Management Policy

Digital Marketing Strategy & Tactics

Campaign Creation Templates

Job Descriptions

Social Media Manager

Community Manager

Copywriter

Visual Storyteller

Digital Marketing Policies

"Don't throw caution to the wind when it comes to how you expect your team to engage with internal and external customers – spell it out so there is no confusion."

~Tisha Holman

When you hire people to join your team, you cannot make the assumption that they will conduct themselves in a way you might see as common sense. You must spell it out, so your expectations are clear and they are accountable to them.

Below you will find the areas you need to draft policies for—outside of a general operations manual. For training purposes, you should create a separate handbook that houses all these policies, so that new employees can sign off on general acknowledgement of them all in the onboarding process.

- Accessibility
- Data, Analytics & Insights Reporting
- Brand Reputation
- Brand Style Guide
- Company Digital Culture & Values
- Cookies & Activity Tracking
- Copyrights & Protections
- Crisis Management
- Data Breach Response
- Data Privacy
- Digital Assets (domain names, email addresses, social media handles, etc.)
- E-Commerce
- Editorial Style Guide
- Email Marketing
- Web Hosting & Content Storage
- Information Technology
- Key Performance Indicator Measurement
- Password Hygiene & Credential Management
- Product Advertisement & Placement
- Search Engine Optimization
- Social Media Conduct
- Social Media (personal use)

Credential Management

A note about password hygiene and credential management. Cybersecurity breaches are getting increasingly sophisticated, so you really do need to do your part to protect your digital assets.

- Use a password manager
- Enforce password history policy
- Enable a maximum password age policy
- Require that passwords meet complexity requirements
- Have a password audit policy
- Have a plan for staff that leaves the organization (passwords & digital assets)
- Never grant staff more access to accounts than what is needed

Crisis Management

"It's handled."

~Olivia Pope

Gone are the days when we have to wait for the 5 o'clock news to get the scoop on bad news. Having a Crisis Management Plan will allow your brand to provide customer service in the digital space for an immediate, personalized response to individual comments, complaints, questions, and reviews online.

The court of public opinion will try to convict those in the digital space before they ever get their day in court. Showing up online has its inherent risks, but those risks certainly don't outweigh the rewards. You just need to be prepared if a digital conundrum lands in your lap.

It is critical that you take a proactive approach to formulating responses and engagement strategies, in addition to each individual message or mention:

- Define the "crisis" - there's levels to this!
- Establish a procedure for assessing the nature and severity of the issue
- Suspend any scheduled content until the mattered is assessed
- Define and communicate roles and responsibilities for all involved parties
- Create a communication plan for all internal and external updates
- Identify the key stakeholders and be sure their contact information is accessible
- Determine what the approval flow will be for the publication of any copy or messaging online
- Plan a post-crisis deconstruction of what occurred so opportunities to strengthen your crisis plan can be identified

Is This Really An Emergency?

While you are triaging whether the situation at hand is truly an emergency, use this list of possible actions that may need to be taken while the situation is evaluated. Routine criticism of general topics that are typical in your industry are not considered an emergency as much as it is something that just needs to be addressed appropriately online. Here are some things to keep in mind as you and your team assess whether you truly have a digital conundrum on your hands:

- Evaluate any existing posts or articles that may contain offensive or insensitive content or verbiage

- Edit, remove, or delete any content that may be harmful or negatively impact your brand
- Involve and notify any relevant department leads or stakeholders about the matter as it pertains to their purview of responsibility
- Stop or pause social media content
- Stop or pause ads or boosted posts
- Stop or pause email marketing newsletters
- Make any needed changes or adjustments to the editorial and social media content calendar to mitigate the issue
- Create new blogs and backlinks to mitigate negative viral content
- Develop and publish any written statements or press releases addressing the matter
- Supply any key stakeholders or publicists with relevant details and talking points for the matter
- Be sure to communicate any changes or updates to staff (especially public facing) so the messaging is unified and consistent
- Take an assessment of what the impact of this situation will be on your brand

Standard Operating Procedures

"Do you run a business, or do you own a job? Whether or not you document your processes and procedures is the answer to the question."

~Tisha Holman

The goal is growth—and these docs prepare you for that journey. Standard Operating Procedures (SOPs) are an integral facet of building a solid, scalable system for your digital strategy efforts. Having SOPs makes it much easier to onboard new people to your team, as they will have the specific recipe for your brand's secret sauce. When everyone on your team is following the same roadmap, the work is getting done the same way.

Content Creation SOP

- Where ideas are sourced (content pillars, launches, events, evergreen content)

- Copywriting workflows and approval process
- Graphic design templates, tools, design guidelines (cross-ref brand guide)
- Video editing template, tools, design guidelines

Content Planning SOP

- Monthly master editorial calendar (blog, email, social media, text, app, ads)
- Calendar review and final approvals

Social Media Management SOP

- Scheduling tools and platform-specific best practices
- Weekly publishing schedule
- Hashtag strategy, mentions, backlinks
- Engagement and Community management workflows (FAQ/Monitoring doc)
- KPI and data tracking (reporting schedules/formats, frequency)

Email Marketing SOP

- Weekly or monthly email planning
- Template library for various campaigns
- Testing and approvals
- List management and segmentation rules
- Definition of KPI's (open rates, CTR, etc.)
- Automation workflows - lead magnets, sales funnels, nurture sequences

Lead Magnet + Sales Funnel SOP

- Lead magnet creation process
- Landing page copy and design workflows
- Email automation setup + tagging
- Lead pathways - (CRM, spreadsheets, etc.)
- Ongoing testing and conversion tracking

Analytics and Reporting SOP

- Toolset (GA, scheduling tools, native platforms)
- KPIs per platform (email, web, social, text, app, ads)
- Reporting format and cadence
- How to analyze, catalyze, and pivot strategy based on the results
- Comprehensive performance summary (monthly, quarterly, annually)

Launch Strategy SOP

- Launch phases (pre-launch, warm-up, promo, close)
- Deliverables by platform
- Timelines and RACI charts (responsible, accountable, consulted, informed)
- Messaging map - CopySignature™ plug and play
- Real-time feedback loop during open cart

Live Event Campaign SOP

- Phases (pre-con, live, post-con)
- Event CopySignature™ + copywriting
- Graphic design templates, tools, design guidelines (cross-ref brand guide)
- Video editing template, tools, design guidelines
- KPI and data tracking (reporting schedules/formats, frequency)

Client Journey SOP

- What happens when a lead becomes a client
- Onboarding process
- Onboarding email flows
- Access - Portal credentials, Community, content
- Client feedback survey workflows
- Testimonial request workflows
- Re-engagement or upsell follow-up

Measuring Success

"Measurement is the connector between intention and impact."

~Tisha Holman

Where are you trying to go? You can't move forward with an unknown goal, and it's worth repeating that what doesn't get measured, doesn't get done. Furthermore, if you aren't seeing an ROI on your efforts in the digital space, then whatever you are doing is a major WOT (waste of time)!

As you begin to determine what success looks like for you online, beware of the "Fatal Attraction," better known as vanity metrics. Vanity metrics are those superfluous data points that don't have a real value in content that converts to cash. Followers, post likes, page views—those kinds of metrics—bear no correlation to the value of your content, any measure of your expertise or thought-leadership, or drive your profitability in the real-world. Sadly enough, there is a large population of people that put a lot of stock into these numbers that are now readily available, and very often purchased, for, well, vanity reasons. I mention this so you do not allow what others may perceive as a small follower count or likes on posts, and cunning algorithms that limit your followers' visibility of your content to get into your head. This vanity metric fixation is the petri dish for imposter syndrome. They have their place as a barometer for how things may be resonating with your audience, but I cannot emphasize enough that big follower counts don't equal success…again, you can literally buy them now.

Establishing Key Performance Indicators (KPIs)

Define the KPIs that make dollars and sense for your bottom line. There should be clear and realistic benchmarks that are success factors for EVERYTHING you do. Your measurement of what success looks like in your business is an important piece of the puzzle that will eventually position you to not just scale, but scale smartly.

There is power in a data-driven strategy, and it is what will differentiate you from others in your industry, because the statistics tell us that 77% of small business owners don't have a strategy, so the odds are pretty high they are just winging it.

Here are a few areas that are a good place to start with what you are measuring from your digital platforms:

- A/B and Multi-Variate testing
- Social listening - can reveal interests, emerging topics, keywords
- Web traffic - visits, bounce rate, geo location, user behavior on your site
- Email - CTR, Open Rate
- Social Media

 ## SIDELINE SIGNAL!

Mindset is such an important part of your success. I want to be sure you are equipped with what you need to win. Sometimes, the conversations you have with yourself can have the greatest influence on your decisions and perceptions. Here are a few positive phrases I'd like you to say to yourself as you establish what your KPIs are going to look like—and revisit them whenever you evaluate the data. Stay encouraged!

"My numbers are not a verdict; they are a compass."

"Clarity in my data is power in my decisions."

"I am building a strategy, not chasing validation."

Monitoring & FAQ Documents

Docs needed to keep your CopySignature™ consistent every time you speak online, no matter who is at the helm and responsible for sharing content.

These docs allow your team to support you without having to tap you on your shoulder to find out what they should say in common scenarios.

General everyday things like lead magnets, links to schedule meetings, details about the services you offer, and links to products.

Attracting Top Tier Talent

"Every high-performing company has the same secret: they treat talent as strategy."

~Tisha Holman

Meet Jason.

Jason's resume was stellar. He had experience with some of the nation's top brands, and his resume highlighted some of the wins he had on those teams. Jason was the brains behind increases in all the metrics that count. He cooly navigated the various questions I asked to assess his ability to handle the rigors of the position I was hiring for. He was charismatic, seemed savvy with the latest trends in content creation, and he was used to being around celebrities, which was important for this opportunity. I thought I had found myself a unicorn. WRONG. Jason ended up being a marketing manager's nightmare. Instead of capturing content at events, he was capturing selfies with talent. Where did the amazing copywriting skills go in the work samples he showed me? Because now he couldn't get a subject and a verb to agree in a sentence to save his life! Creative content ideas and an awareness of the latest trends? Nowhere to be found. What had I done? And if you've ever been a leader in a corporate setting, you know hiring is far less complicated than firing. It took about three months, but I was eventually able to release Jason to his next opportunity. Whew!

Jason was the reason I took a step back to re-evaluate my hiring methods, beef up the situational questions I asked, and create a process that was more practical and really demonstrated someone's potential contribution to the vision of the team. When it comes to your digital marketing and brand presence, you need a strategic partner, not just a "doer" who carries out tasks on a checklist.

To keep our conversation as evergreen as possible, I am going to share roles you'll need to fill to support your digital marketing efforts, along with ten traits you should look for in the person you choose to hire.

Community Managers

1. Emotional intelligence – ability to read the room and respond with tact.
2. Crisis communication – can de-escalate negativity while protecting brand reputation.
3. Relationship-builder – turns followers into brand advocates.
4. Analytical mindset – knows how to interpret engagement data to improve.
5. Empathy-driven tone – connects on a human level.
6. Conflict resolution – balances fairness with firmness.
7. Cultural awareness – sensitive to diverse audiences.
8. Consistency & presence – reliable daily engagement.
9. Storytelling chops – frames responses as mini brand narratives.

10. Resilient under pressure – thrives even when comments get messy.

Copywriters

1. Conversion-focused writing – every word drives action.
2. Voice chameleon – adapts tone to match brand personality seamlessly.
3. Clarity + punch – makes the complex sound simple and compelling.
4. SEO literacy – knows how to write for humans and algorithms.
5. Persuasion psychology – understands triggers that move people to buy.
6. Curiosity-driven researcher – digs deep for insights before writing.
7. Creative agility – can write ads, emails, captions, and long-form all at a high level.
8. Data-informed – A/B testing mindset, knows what works in-market.
9. Narrative structure – builds tension, release, and payoff.
10. Unapologetically bold – avoids generic copy, goes straight for impact.

Graphic Designers

1. Brand fidelity – translates strategy into visual identity.
2. Conceptual thinker – doesn't just decorate, but communicates meaning.
3. UX awareness – design that's functional and intuitive, not just pretty.
4. Strong typographic skills – understands hierarchy and readability.
5. Creative originality – avoids templates; produces scroll-stopping work.
6. Motion & multimedia fluency – static, video, and animation flexibility.
7. Collaborative mindset – works seamlessly with copywriters/storytellers.
8. Trend-aware but timeless – balances fresh and lasting design.
9. Fast execution – can produce high-quality work at speed.
10. Eye for detail – pixel-perfect and consistent across platforms.

Digital Storytellers (not the same as a videographer)

1. Narrative instinct – knows how to craft a story arc visually.
2. Technical mastery – camera, lighting, audio, editing at pro level.
3. Creative director's eye – frames scenes that evoke emotion.
4. Agility in formats – Reels, YouTube, event recaps, brand films.
5. Sound design sensitivity – understands audio as half the experience.
6. Post-production wizardry – color grading, pacing, storytelling in edits.
7. Marketing literacy – creates content that serves business objectives.
8. On-the-spot adaptability – can pivot when shoots don't go as planned.
9. Collaborative flow – works smoothly with writers, designers, and marketers.
10. Visionary mindset – sees beyond "content" into cultural impact.

Podcast Editor/Producer

1. Audio engineering excellence – clean, professional, immersive sound.
2. Story flow design – edits for rhythm, engagement, and emotional pacing.
3. Interview coaching ability – helps hosts and guests shine.
4. Creative sound scaping – music, transitions, ambiance that enhances.
5. Detail-obsessed – removes filler words, distractions, noise.
6. Technical troubleshooting – solves mic, recording, and software issues fast.
7. Distribution savvy – knows platforms, tagging, and SEO for podcast reach.
8. Marketing partnership – collaborates to turn episodes into promos/snippets.
9. Deadline discipline – delivers consistently, no excuses.
10. Listener-first lens – optimizes every decision for the end-user's experience.

Social Media Manager

1. Strategic planner – aligns daily content with big-picture business goals.

2. Data-obsessed – measures, interprets, and pivots based on analytics.

3. Trend spotter – taps into culture before it peaks.

4. Creative content ideation – generates fresh, on-brand campaign ideas.

5. Platform fluency – deep knowledge of algorithms and best practices.

6. Community connector – builds genuine engagement, not vanity metrics.

7. Copy & visual coordination – understands the marriage of words and design.

8. Crisis manager – protects the brand in high-stakes social moments.

9. Agile executor – balances speed with strategy.

10. Big-picture marketer – sees social as one piece of the funnel, not the whole.

I understand the challenges that come along with expanding your team and what growing to scale can entail. Budget constraints, having the proper processes in place so they are truly able to function, and then a lack of understanding of the tasks these roles should own— it can all be so daunting. Don't be that person trying to cram all of these job descriptions into one underpaid and overworked person! I have seen it time and time again, and the caveat I will share is that this only breeds high attrition and unhappy people.

There is also AI to consider. The technology is advancing so quickly, and people are finding new ways to "hire AI" in their organizations. We'll touch on this more later, for now, I'll just say be cautious at removing humanity and heart too far away from your organization chart.

TIME OUT!

Here is a scorecard you can use to help you rate candidates during the interview process. Build your questions around these categories. Make adjustments as you see fit, and may the best man win!

Category Description	Criteria	Points Possible
Strategic Thinking & Problem-Solving	• Understands the big picture, not just their lane • Can analyze goals and propose smart, creative solutions • Anticipates issues before they arise • Aligns execution with business objectives	20
Creativity & Innovation	• Demonstrates originality in ideas, campaigns, and content • Pushes boundaries while staying brand appropriate • Can translate concepts into engaging, fresh outputs • Resourceful and adaptable under constraints	20
Technical Competence	• Mastery of role-specific tools/software/platforms • Keeps up with industry trends and updates • Can troubleshoot independently • Applies best practices consistently	20

Communication & Collaboration	<ul><li>Clear and professional communicator</li><li>Strong active listener, can take and implement feedback</li><li>Plays well with cross-functional teams</li><li>Able to translate complex ideas into digestible language</li></ul>	15
Reliability & Accountability	<ul><li>Meets deadlines consistently</li><li>Owns their work — celebrates wins and learns from misses</li><li>Manages multiple priorities without excuses</li><li>Transparent in progress and reporting</li></ul>	15
Growth Mindset & Adaptability	<ul><li>Proactively seeks learning opportunities</li><li>Comfortable with change and new challenges</li><li>Welcomes constructive criticism</li><li>Continuously levels up their craft</li></ul>	10

Protecting Bright Ideas

"When you start to become known for disruptive innovation ...people are going to steal your stuff."

~Tisha Holman

Before we get started here, please allow me to give a bit of a disclaimer. I'm not a lawyer. This is not legal advice. Talk to your lawyer to identify the best course of action for you and your business.

Ok, now that we've got that out of the way…

This is a playbook, right? We are going to look at this chapter as our plan for building a strong defensive line for your business and intellectual property.

The best example I can share of the importance of copywriting and/or trademarking your intellectual property is a personal one. My story is a cautionary tale, and I hope you take serious heed to the lesson that can be learned here. This chapter isn't going to be long, but it is probably one of the most important chapters in this playbook.

Before I tell my story, let's define a couple of important terms.

Intellectual Property - The Oxford dictionary defines intellectual property as "a work or invention that is the result of creativity, such as a manuscript or a design, to which one has rights and for which one may apply for a patent, copyright, trademark, etc."

Copyright - A copyright is a federally granted property right that protects rights holders from certain unauthorized uses of their original works of authorship. Copyrightable works include literary, dramatic, musical, and artistic works such as books, plays, music, lyrics, paintings, sculptures, video games, movies, sound recordings, and software. (United States Patent and Trademark Office)

The USPTO makes a point of clarification about copyrights that I want to share with you: "Copyright protection does not extend to ideas, procedures, processes, systems, methods of operation, concepts, principles, or discoveries. Copyright protects only the expression of an idea, not the idea itself. This principle, sometimes called the "idea-expression dichotomy," ensures that protection will extend only to the original elements that the author has contributed to a work, not to the work's underlying ideas, which remain freely available to the public."

Trademark - A trademark can be any word, phrase, symbol, design, or combination of these things that identifies your goods or services. It's how customers recognize you in the marketplace and distinguish you from your competitors.

A trademark:

- Identifies the source of your goods or services.
- Provides legal protection for your brand.
- Helps you guard against counterfeiting and fraud.

Licensing - The Book of Tisha definition is contractually granting permission to another entity to use your copyrighted, trademarked, or patented intellectual property.

Patent - A patent gives you, the inventor, the right to "exclude others from making, using, offering for sale, or selling" an invention or "importing" it into the U.S.A.

Story time.

I was an entrepreneur before I truly understood what an entrepreneur was. When I was a kid no more than seven or eight years old, sometimes my aunt and uncle would come to visit us for the weekend. They slept in my bedroom, and I would invade—I mean sleep in the bed with my Nana, and I was a horrible sleeper! It was during those times that I transformed into the proprietor of The Grand Luxury Hotel. I don't recall how I came up with that name; I guess we can suffice to say that I have always liked nice things. I would set my little table up at the door to "check them in," take their luggage to their "suite," and ensure they experienced stellar hospitality for the entirety of their stay. Fun times.

Fast forward to my teenage years. To this day, my high school junior prom was one of the worst events I have attended. We were the class of 2000, and in my determination to make sure we went out with a bang, I ran for senior class vice president, because that person chaired the senior ball committee, and I wanted to make sure things were done right this time! Our senior ball was held at a beautiful country club, and it was definitely a night to remember! Who knew that chain of events would lead to what eventually became Tisha Holman Events, a brand that would take me to some of the most beautiful destinations in the world, planning weddings, executing logistics for global events, print magazine features, and regular appearances on my local TV networks!!

Mind Your Business is and continues to amaze me. I am not always good at celebrating my own accomplishments, but I am truly proud of the work I am doing to help business owners like yourself grow something amazing that you too can be proud of. Modern-day ways of business have people making goals to be an "overnight success" and they skip over important elements of the foundation their business should be built upon.

Mind Your Business - what a clever name, right?

I received a phone call from a producer one day who excitedly shared an opportunity to be a part of a new reality show where a "business powerhouse" was going to come in and transform your business to prime you for that elusive "next level" people often talk about. There were two things that unfortunately took me out of the running to be potentially cast on this show. First, she had found me through the media around Tisha Holman Events, so she didn't realize that she had a digital marketing strategist on the line, not an event planner and designer. Second, they wanted the person to have a brick-and-mortar building—being a newly established service business, I worked remotely, as did the members of my team. The producer was still intrigued and wanted to learn more about what a digital marketing strategist does. As I began to explain it to her, in true reality show producer fashion, she was probing for the salacious parts of working together—she wanted to hear about the drama. No ma'am. I proudly explained to her that I am not the kind of leader or business owner who would create that type of company culture. I had done my time in toxic workplaces; there is no way I was going to build one of my own. She asked me the name of the business, and guys let me tell you this lady was beside herself. She thought the name Mind Your Business was so clever and creative, I mean, like really gushing on about it. Ok, I guess? Glad you like the name. Ultimately, we landed on the fact that I was not going to be a good fit for the show, exchanged pleasantries, and ended the call.

Six months later, OWN—yes, the Oprah Winfrey Network—dropped a new show called Mind Your Business with Mahisha. It was a new cutting-edge reality show, where entrepreneur and beauty founder, Mahisha Dellinger would be using her experience and business savvy to whip businesses into shape. I almost tripped over my own feet looking for the notebook I was writing in during my conversation with that producer because I knew I had written down the name of the show during that phone call. As you can probably guess, the show originally had a totally different name. I was sick to my stomach. The name wasn't trademarked, but there was an argument there since I had established that name first in the marketplace, and the possibility of brand confusion was definitely possible. Mind Your Business and Tisha Holman - Mind Your Business with Mahisha. Ehhh. So, what did I do next? Nothing. I didn't think that little old me would stand a chance going up against what would surely be a team of high-powered attorneys that represented the network, even though I likely could have prevailed in that case.

You would think I would have learned my lesson from that? Of course not.

Fast forward some years, and in a casual search to find my own page, I discovered that there was someone out there also offering digital marketing services, with the name Mind Your Business! Completely different target market, but the same concept. OH EM GEEEEEE!! Long, frustrating story short, we had to land a shared use agreement of the trademark - and thankfully, the whole ordeal led them to abandon the use of the name, so it's just me out there. Lesson all the way learned. The harsh reality of the fact that I could have lost use of the name of my beloved business, due to my own inaction, still makes me a little queasy. Don't take your bright ideas for granted.

Well friends, this was cathartic—I have never told this story to anyone before—and I must say it feels good to be able to share this cautionary tale so that you can avoid experiencing something like this.

The moral of this story is a direct call to immediate action:

PROTECT YOUR STUFF! NOW.

To swing back to the situation with OWN; I want to call out that my reasoning for not wanting to pursue legal action on that producer stealing my name was a form of imposter syndrome. The fact of the matter is, I was fully entitled to stand strong in the fight for what was mine; the opponent didn't matter. Right is right, and what that producer did was wrong. Full stop. Maybe I'll tell Oprah this story over brunch one of these days? You never know!

Let's lean back into the theme of the playbook as I share some things I want you to keep in mind as you do your due diligence to protect your bright ideas. I'm calling a time-out so we can talk defense in this part of the game!

TIME OUT!

1. Identify the Plays Worth Protecting (Clarity). Highlight the intellectual property that is truly your proprietary secret sauce vs. what's just day-to-day content.

- Audit your assets: frameworks, logos, taglines, courses, programs, content, podcasts.
- Ask: "If someone copied this tomorrow, would it compromise my brand, revenue, or reputation?"

2. Assign the Right Defense (Copyright vs. Trademark vs. Patent). Show how each type of protection works like a different defensive position on the field.

- Copyright = your creative works (books, videos, podcasts, graphics, copy).
- Trademark = your brand identifiers (business name, program names, logos, taglines).
- Patent = inventions or unique processes.

3. File Your Plays Properly (External Protection) Make this step feel like putting the official stamp on your playbook so no one else can run your plays.

- Copyright: Register with the U.S. Copyright Office.
- Trademark: File through USPTO or work with an IP attorney.
- Document: Keep dated drafts, contracts, and ownership agreements.

4. Guard the Locker Room (Internal Protection) Boundaries have to be in place for your own team as well.

- NDAs for contractors and collaborators.
- Clear ownership clauses in contracts.

- Password-protected systems, limited access, and role-based permissions.

5. Call the Fouls (Enforcement). Don't let infractions slide.

- Monitor: Google alerts, social listening tools, competitor checks.
- Respond: Cease-and-desist letters, attorney follow-ups.

6. Keep the Playbook Updated (Futureproofing). Build protecting your bright ideas into the standard operating rhythm for your company.

- Reassess protections as you launch new programs, offers, or frameworks.
- Update trademarks as you grow.

The Strategy

"Your strategy is not your plan. The strategy is your why, tactics are how you will make it happen."

~*Tisha Holman*

We have all heard those staggering statistics about the failure rate of small businesses. According to the Bureau of Labor Statistics, 50% of small businesses do not make it past the five-year mark. Why is that? I wouldn't say that these businesses are not making it because they weren't passionate about their work or didn't work hard; the failure comes because they didn't work smart enough. One of the most prevalent examples of this that I see in the digital space is the constant focus on beating the latest algorithm and keeping up with the current trends, as opposed to aligning their content plan with the goals of their business.

Maybe you can relate? Have you spent months obsessing over your content? You have tried everything, every tool, every trend—but all you feel is burned out and overwhelmed—and the only results you are seeing are flat sales and stagnant growth. Perhaps you have an understanding of the "how" (what to post, when to send those emails), but, unfortunately, the "why" is escaping you because you never stopped to identify what exactly you were trying to achieve and how it connects to your bigger vision.

In this chapter, you are going to learn the critical difference between strategy and tactics and why conflating the two is going to lead to you joining the ranks of the business owners who close up shop before they ever got a chance to really shine.

Having a strong, intentional strategy in place is your filter for every decision, specifically every marketing decision that you make in your business. It is how you ensure that every move you make is something that is driving systems and success in your business. The bottom line is, if you don't know your "why", there is no measure of hustle, grind, vibes, or viral content that will position you for sustainable success and profits—the place you really want to be.

There is a danger in skipping strategy because you end up "measuring" success by your activity, not actual results, and it becomes the perfect opportunity for impostor syndrome to rear its ugly head. Your effort and the numbers won't match, making it easy for you to say that digital marketing doesn't work and is a waste of time.

Let's look a little deeper into defining strategy and tactics. I want to make sure the difference between them is crystal clear so that when you begin working on yours, you are set up for success.

Strategy

Most business owners start with action as opposed to being strategy-first and purpose-driven. The shift from being a business owner that is trapped in a cycle of reactive marketing means recognizing a few things that you are likely guilty of that have to stop now. Being a business owner who leads strategy-first will be what helps you and your team know exactly what to focus on and what to ignore, and you stop wasting energy on things that do not serve your goals.

Until you stop jumping on the latest platform because "everyone else is doing it", changing course every time a self-proclaimed guru drops a new formula, and measuring success by vanity metrics instead of what really matters most, there's not a tactic in the world that will lead you to the success that serious business owners get to enjoy.

Your strategy should not be a laundry list of action items disguised as goals. Your first order of business in the development of your strategy is to clarify what you are working toward and what the ultimate goal is.

Guiding Questions:

1. What are your profit goals?
2. What space in the marketplace do I want to own, and why is it important now?
3. Am I building something that resonates with my Perfect M.A.T.C.H.™?
4. What problem will I be known for solving expertly, at the highest level?
5. What are the non-negotiable outcomes I want to achieve over the next 12-18 months?

6. What is the transformation that you want your clients to experience or achieve?

Once your vision is clear, it is time to define what tangible success looks like. Your strategy will become a real thing once it's attached to a measurable outcome. If you can't measure it, you can't manage it and what doesn't get measured, doesn't get done.

Your next move will be to establish strategic anchors that will serve as the core areas of focus that get you to the goal. Creating strategic anchors will allow you to stay on track toward achieving your strategic plans and ensure that you create a tactical plan for every goal that you want to accomplish. This is the way your content doesn't fall into the trap of turning into "random acts of marketing" that are anything but kind to the success of your company. Allow me to suggest a few strategic anchors that you can leverage to get your wheels turning. Leaning in on these anchors will undoubtedly lead to tactics that will yield movement in the areas that matter most.

Strategic Anchors:
- Visibility: Increase awareness of your brand through organic and eventually paid content
- Authority: Establish credibility through thought leadership and exposure through public relations
- Conversion: Cha-Ching! Optimize campaigns to maximize your ROI
- Retention: Build community, loyalty and lifetime clients

Tactics

Execution-driven

Short-term actions

Flexible and adaptable

The biggest brands out there are extremely intentional about everything they do, especially marketing. Do you remember during the pandemic, when DJ D-Nice opened the doors of Club Quarantine on Instagram Live? All of our favorite A-list celebrities and 250K others were all in VIP together, enjoying the universal connection of music as the salve we didn't know we needed as we navigated the isolation of the lockdown. DJ D-Nice did what all brands in demand do: he became the answer to the problem his audience had but that wasn't an accidental accomplishment. During the preceding two weeks, DJ D-Nice leveraged the power of his network to get the word out about what was coming to Instagram Live in a way that had yet to be done before. The likes of Oprah, Michelle Obama, Mark Zuckerberg, Drake, The Rock, Quincy Jones, and more entered through the virtual velvet ropes of that magical space, but it was not happenstance. The courage to ask his "friends" for a favor led to a movement that would lead to brand deals and opportunities he could have never imagined. It is the power of implementing tactics that are aligned with the goals of your business; with consistency and intentionality, you position yourself to receive more than you planned for.

Tactics are in service to strategy, so they can change often. Think of it like GPS. Your destination is fixed (strategy), but depending on traffic, road closures, etc., the routes can change to ensure you get to where you want to go in the most efficient way (tactics).

Resisting The Fatal Attraction

Trending topics, new shiny tools, and platforms can be very enticing, which is why you have to create a filter for what you choose to do online. There are going to be some things that simply will not resonate with your audience or align with the values of your brand.

A few questions to ask before you decide to ride the wave of the latest trending topic:

- Does it align with our overall strategic plan?
- Does it move you closer to our defined objectives?
- Does it fit within our current strategic anchors?
- Can we measure its impact clearly?

If the answer to any one of these is "no", then it's a distraction and a tactic not worth implementing.

It is like a fatal attraction: the connection seemed like a good idea at first—even fun—but you soon realize that all it did was take you out of alignment with the path you were supposed to take, bringing you unwanted grief and people who aren't your Perfect M.A.T.C.H.™ therefore your marketing efforts don't resonate them, so they don't convert to cash....see where I'm going with this? Don't fall for it.

Let me show you some examples of what strategic anchors and aligned tactics look like in action:

Strategic Anchor	Aligned Tactics
Visibility	Instagram Reels, LinkedIn Lives, SEO blog content
Authority	Podcasting (Yours and guests on others), speaking engagements, media pitches
Conversion	Systems and Sales funnel optimization, ads/retargeting, trip wires
Retention	Loyalty programs, personalized email journeys, customized offers

To further drive this concept home, let me give you an example that integrates a specific goal with strategic anchors and tactics that lead to momentum in the marketplace.

Goal: A coaching business wants to double revenue by the end of the year

Strategy:

- Establish the brand as the top choice for mid-level professionals who are ready to make the jump into entrepreneurship.
- Build a scalable digital marketing ecosystem to support consistent client leads that convert.

Tactics:

- Launch a LinkedIn thought leadership campaign (visibility)
- Build an automated email nurture sequence for new leads (conversion)
- Run a targeted ad campaign to attract new audiences (visibility + conversion)
- Leveraging PR tactics, be a guest on a podcast that allows you to get in front of new audiences to demonstrate your expertise. Negotiate the ability to send an offer to their email list (authority + retention)

Strategy – The why and the destination	Tactics – The how and the route
Sets the vision and direction	Executes the strategy step-by-step
Long-term, focused on the big picture	Short-term, flexible, and can change often
Defines what success looks like	Details how to achieve success
Guides decisions and priorities	Lives in processes, systems, workflows,

TIME OUT!

1. What are you currently doing in your marketing that feels random or disconnected?

2. What is the one clear outcome you want from your marketing over the next 6 months?

3. Which tactics are you using that don't align with that outcome?

4. What does success actually look like for you?

Unlikely Mentors:
What The Ritz-Carlton and Disney
Teach Us About Operational
Excellence

When most entrepreneurs think about mentors, they picture industry experts, consultants, or business icons. Rarely do they look to hospitality giants for guidance. But if you want to understand operational excellence that feels seamless, human, and unforgettable, there are no better teachers than The Ritz-Carlton Hotel and Disney. These companies have mastered radical hospitality at a level so profound that their operational standards have become global benchmarks. They don't just serve customers—they design experiences, and every operational decision supports that mission with precision.

The Ritz-Carlton is world-renowned not simply because of luxury, but because of systems-backed service. Their commitment to excellence is built into their operations at every layer—from employee empowerment to daily standards of performance. One of their most famous operational strategies is the $2,000 rule, which allows any employee, at any level, to spend up to $2,000 to resolve a guest issue without asking for permission. This is not about the money; it's about empowerment, trust, and speed of execution. That kind of autonomy requires meticulous training, clear expectations, and a culture where excellence is non-negotiable. Their teams don't guess what great service looks like; they are trained, rehearsed, and prepared to deliver it consistently.

Equally important is The Ritz-Carlton's practice of the Daily Lineup, where staff meet every day to review service standards, share wins, and reinforce the brand's values. It's operational muscle memory—repetition that ensures excellence isn't an accident but a predictable outcome. In other words, The Ritz-Carlton treats exceptional service the way high-performing organizations treat mission-critical operations: with clarity, rituals, and accountability.

Disney operates with the same level of intentionality, but on a scale few organizations ever reach. Disney doesn't simply entertain—they engineer magic. Their success is built on what they call "backstage and onstage" operations, a distinction that clarifies exactly what guests should—and should never—see. Every cast member, from ride operators to street sweepers, understands that they are not employees; they are performers contributing to a narrative. That story-driven approach shapes everything from cleanliness protocols to how directions are given in the parks.

Disney's operational excellence is also rooted in anticipatory service. Their teams are trained to solve problems before guests know they exist. Trash cans are placed exactly 27 steps apart based on guest behavior studies. Lines are engineered to feel shorter through interactive design. Even the soundtrack transitions are mapped to ensure emotional continuity as guests move through the park. Nothing is left to chance. Every operational choice is a strategic one.

What makes both The Ritz-Carlton and Disney powerful "unlikely mentors" is this: they do not rely on talent alone—they rely on systems that create predictability, emotional connection, and brand loyalty. These organizations understand that excellence is not an act of heroism; it is an act of design. Their operations make the extraordinary feel easy, and that is the real lesson.

In your business, you may not be serving luxury travelers or creating theme park magic. But you are creating experiences. And when you understand that every touchpoint—every process, every response, every system—is a chance to build trust and exceed expectations, you elevate from being a service provider to being a brand people remember.

Section Summary: Operations

Action Tasks

1. Map Your Client Journey: Document every step from first touchpoint to final deliverable. Identify friction points or gaps.

2. Systemize Top 3 Processes: Choose the three most repeated tasks and create SOPs for them this week.

3. Eliminate Operational Clutter: Identify five tools, subscriptions, or processes you no longer use. Cancel or consolidate them.

Prompts

- Where is your client experience breaking down or becoming inconsistent?
- If you stepped away for 30 days, what would immediately fall apart in your business?
- Which recurring tasks could be delegated or automated to free you up for strategy and leadership?

Exercises

- Bottleneck Hunt:

    Write out every step in a current project. Circle the tasks that:
    - Take too long
    - Require you personally to complete.
    - Create frustration for clients or team members.

These are your immediate priorities for delegation or improvement.

- Freedom Metric Challenge:

    Create a KPI that measures how many hours you personally spend on delivery vs. growth activities.

Goal: Reduce delivery hours by 25% in the next quarter.

Revenue and Reach

REVENUE & REACH

"If it doesn't make dollars, it doesn't make sense."

~*Tisha Holman*

R evenue & Reach is the part of the C.O.R.E.™ Model that is all about monetizing with intention and amplifying with precision. The fact of the matter is, if you want consistent growth without chasing trends and fleeting moments online, you need to curate an ecosystem that is purposeful and profitable.

This is where most high-achieving service providers hit the wall, and hit it hard. You've built a solid brand, and you know your expertise is undeniable, but you're starting to feel like you're on a content treadmill that's not really taking you anywhere. You're just floating between launches, live events, and referrals without a strategy that makes dollars and sense for your business. WHEW!

What Revenue & Reach Really Mean

Revenue & Reach are interconnected; one without the other creates an imbalance in the rhythm and flow of your business. Revenue goes far beyond selling; it is also the creation of sustainable systems that align with your brand promise, sales psychology, and the capacity of your team. Pairing this with a targeted and intentional visibility plan that speaks to your Perfect MATCH™, in the right way, at the right time, will be what makes your digital presence profitable. The goal is for you to begin owning your space online with the confidence and clarity that helps you convert to cash consistently.

Part 1: Revenue – The Right Stuff!

Let's start with revenue because, well, you're in business to make money, right? We can come up with all kinds of strategies, tactics, and branding to discover your Perfect M.A.T.C.H.™, but if you don't have a viable offer for them to opt into, it is all for nothing. Your offer suite, pricing model, and client conversion systems are the heartbeat of your brand's sustainability and scalability.

There is a cadre of revenue activators that I like to call…ahem (in my Vanessa Williams voice) "The Right Stuff" that you must master so you can monetize at a high level:

- The Right Audience (Perfect M.A.T.C.H.™) - Serve those ready, willing, and able to invest in the transformation you offer.
- The Right Message (CopySignature™) - The bespoke language that speaks to their desires, fears, and outcomes.
- The Right Model - How you structure and deliver your offers.
- The Right Metrics - Key Performance Indicators that actually matter for revenue growth.

- The Right Amplifiers - Systems that expand revenue by letting you work smarter as opposed to harder.

The Right Stuff

AUDIENCE	MESSAGE	MODEL	METRICS	AMPLIFIERS
The right audience fuels the machine.	The right message creates momentum,	The right model ensures sustainability.	The right metrics guide decision-making.	The right amplifiers keep things moving at full speed.

The right audience fuels the machine.

The right message creates momentum,

The right model ensures sustainability.

The right metrics guide decision-making.

The right amplifiers keep things moving at full speed, sans the burnout.

We have talked quite a bit about alignment—these are the gears that you have to constantly shift in the right direction, but remember, when the gears are out of alignment, you're grinding and therefore not making any progress.

SIDELINE SIGNAL!

⇒ Which activator is your strongest right now?

⇒ Which one is holding your revenue back the most?

⇒ What's one step you can take this week to level up your weakest area?

The Foundation: A Strategic Offer Suite

A high-performing small business doesn't offer everything to everyone. Your best outcomes are going to be when you start operating from a place of strategic clarity, with specific offers that meet your audience exactly where they are–without overwhelming them and draining your resources, time, and money. Now you may be thinking, "Tisha, what does this have to do with my digital marketing strategy?" To that, I would tell you again, I'm a different kind of digital marketing strategist because I am concerned with your business in its totality. That is the way I can help you build a brand and a strategy that moves your business forward. Recall I said earlier that confused minds don't decide. Your offer, your expertise, and the transformation you provide need to be obvious, so the path is clear.

Your offer suite needs to be:

- Aligned with your expertise and client transformation pathway
- Diversified in format or method of access (done-for-you, coaching, VIP days, digital courses, etc.)
- Structured to guide a buyer through a logical journey

The Psychology of Pricing

Your content needs to convert to cash. Every call to action may not be directly transactional, but every call to action should have a goal to put buyers on the journey into your ecosystem. Pricing becomes mission-critical because undercharging is a symptom of unclear value articulation and misaligned positioning. Let's keep it real. Low prices tend to equal a lower commitment (but higher maintenance), and higher prices tend to represent a higher investment in the outcome of the work you will do together. Transparently, I have worked a lot harder for a client who paid $500 and didn't have a true respect for my expertise than the one who paid $15K, saw my value, and was ready to experience a scaled transformation in their life and business. The Perfect M.A.T.C.H.™ is so important!

Your pricing should reflect:

- The magnitude of transformation you provide
- The sophistication level of your ideal client
- The cost to deliver the service at scale (team, tools, time)
- Your long-term profit goals, not just short-term cash flow

Your prices are a positioning signal that communicates your realization of the value and expertise you bring to the conversation—so govern yourself accordingly. This is an area where you have to be watchful that ole impostor syndrome won't come creeping up on you. Our views and mindset about money can be a very layered and complicated topic that we don't realize has an impact on many aspects of life and business. Refer back to the Perfect MATCH™ framework—the H represents clients who have the budget and boldness to invest in themselves. Develop a spirit of boldness in your pricing strategy. After all, one of the best perks of entrepreneurship is the fact that you literally have the power to design the life you want to live! Stop negotiating with people who don't see your value and start speaking to people who expect to pay for expertise and excellence.

TIME OUT!

Your mindset about money is often a mirror that reflects what you think you deserve, and the value that your clients get from working with you.

Let's connect it to The C.O.R.E.™ Model:

Clarity: If you don't believe in the value of your offer, your messaging will always sound uncertain or apologetic.

Operations: A scarcity mindset prevents you from investing in systems and people that can help you scale.

Revenue & Reach: Pricing decisions are not just about numbers; they are a reflection of what you think your expertise is worth.

Evaluation: Fear of data often masks the fear of facing—and confronting—the financial truths in your business.

Point of reflection: Which C.O.R.E.™ area is most affected by your current money mindset?

Well-Rounded Revenue

While high-ticket may be your bread and butter, don't ignore the power of building multiple offer streams within your business:

- Signature high-ticket programs

- Done-for-you retainers or project-based services
- Leveraged group or self-guided digital programs
- Paid consultations
- Live event and workshops
- Subscription/membership options for recurring income

The beauty here is that by leveraging the power of the C.O.R.E.™ Model, you can choose the right mix based on your overall goals and operational capacity.

Sales Systems That Don't Suck The Life Out Of You

Selling should not feel like some daunting, exhausting process that you dread doing. You need an infrastructure that nurtures and converts leads while you mind your business—see what I did there? What is awesome is when your message, pricing, and processes are aligned, sales become an invitation, not a chase.

Your Revenue system should include:
- A lead qualification flow (quiz funnel, mini lessons, checklists)
- Value-driven sales emails (not just pitch-heavy e-blasts)
- Pre-selling content that educates and elevates
- A client enrollment process that closes confidently

The game changer will be when you tie each magnet to a specific offer—your content should connect and convert to cash. That's how you build a Reach to Revenue Pipeline.

Producing content does not equate to reach. There are a lot of folks out there on those digital highways and byways who are loud, and their content only lands because they are consistent. Try this clear, repeatable framework for execution. It will help you stay on track and make progress inevitable

Magnetic Market Positioning

Your CopySignature™ and Perfect M.A.T.C.H.™ frameworks are the combination of the secret sauce that powers this step. The outcome of this strategic positioning is how people say: "I felt like you were talking directly to me." ...because you are.

MAGNETIC REACH = SPECIFIC MESSAGE + CLEAR TRANSFORMATION + CONSISTENT CONTENT

Platform Power Plays

Every brand doesn't need to be on every platform; in fact, you would be wiser not to be. However, just for SEO purposes, grab your social media handles even if you don't plan to have a significant presence on that platform, and go all in where your Perfect MATCH™ hangs out and consumes content.

As of the writing of this playbook, here are the key platforms you should be focusing on as a small business owner. I didn't include Facebook—not saying there is no value there, but the algorithm is so *nuanced there that organic reach has become a slippery slope. Facebook is a great space to run ads, just be sure you have a strategy, and remember your mileage may vary.

No matter where you land with the platforms on which you will focus, make sure your C.O.R.E.™ is strong.

Platform	Strength	Best For
LinkedIn	Authority, B2B sales, speaking leads	Service-based experts, corporate/executives
Instagram	Visibility, community, brand story	Personality-led service brands
YouTube	Long-form trust, search visibility	Evergreen content, lead magnets
Email	Nurture, conversion, retention	Monetization and brand loyalty
Podcast	Intimacy, authority, long-game value	Thought leadership + ecosystem building

 **SIDELINE SIGNAL!**

Need a few suggestions for lead magnets? Here you go!

- Quiz funnels (like your CopySignature™ Score or Perfect MATCH Profiler)
- Checklists or cheat sheets (high-value, low-barrier
- Mini-audio lessons, templates, or toolkits
- Webinar replays or video series (educate & pitch)

That means building your digital footprint with intention:

- Be Google-able (consistent use of your CopySignature™, proper alt-tags, metadata, etc.
- Get featured (traditional media and PR should be a part of your strategy)

- Once you get BRANDED™ - remain consistent (repeatable visuals/language, frameworks, IP
- Repurpose content that connects

  (Blog > YouTube > Instagram > Email)

THE RESULT: PREDICTABLE PROFITS AND REPEATABLE WINS

When your Revenue & Reach ecosystem is dialed in:

- Your messaging is magnetic, and they will come to you hot and ready to buy
- You're not reliant on one launch, platform, or person to bring cash flow into the business because your leads are solid and they come in like clockwork.
- You gain creative freedom because cash flow is systemized.
- Because your content and your cash flow are systemized, you finally get to focus on your zone of genius and not reactive marketing tactics.

PRACTICE DRILL:

Audit your current Revenue & Reach flow. Answer honestly:

- Are your offers designed for scale or survival?
- Is your pricing signaling your true value?
- Do your visibility efforts lead to sales or just vanity metrics?
- Do you have a system that works while you sleep?

Your responses to these questions will help guide and determine where your focus should be.

Streamlining Your Marketing Technology Stack

"A simplified tech stack is a power-move that eliminates wasted time and random acts of marketing."

~Tisha Holman

The software you use to run your digital marketing efforts and really your business overall is an area that definitely needs to make dollars and sense for your bottom line.

Story time.

I was contracted by a global faith-based organization to essentially give their entire approach to digital marketing a makeover…a big makeover. You would be surprised how many huge corporations run like fledgling start-ups. The people on the team in this organization were loyal, but not necessarily skilled. When I got access to all of their systems, evaluating where improvements can be made was a challenge I was more than up for. An intuitive stack of marketing tools is what keeps teams intact. Even with well-documented processes and great systems, if you have rusty tools in the box, you might as well not have gone through the trouble of creating solid processes and systems because the entire thing will be disjointed.

If you can believe it, this organization was using 10 different software systems to run their digital marketing. I was astounded. I balked at the idea of having to maintain login credentials for that many different systems. I shuddered at what it would be like for me to keep up with new passwords as old ones expired at staggered intervals. Worst of all, the expenditure of this wasteful line item was like the Achilles heel of the department budget.

Once I got underneath the hood of the operations in the department, I was able to do a thorough SWOT analysis to expose the areas that needed my attention most. I conducted intentional research and did several demos with representatives from various software companies to determine both the capabilities of their tools and where the gaps existed for smooth implementation.

I find teams run more efficaciously (the spelling bee champ in me really loves this word) when the number of different software tools is minimal, and the tools themselves are robust and cover several interconnected functionalities of the tasks you need them to perform—this makes automation of the amazing processes you have created much simpler to put into practice, and easier for your team to manage.

When all was said and done, those 10 systems were reduced to four, with a total cost savings of $30K annually in the department. With that implementation pending, I was able to begin swift work on building a strong C.O.R.E.™ for the company's digital marketing—this was an amazing start!

From social media scheduling and email automation to analytics, funnels, and customer relationship management, there's a tool for everything, and often, too many tools for everything. At first glance, this abundance of options feels empowering. But as businesses grow, what starts as a handful of smart solutions often turns into a chaotic tech ecosystem that's expensive, inefficient, and impossible to manage. Instead of running your marketing with precision, you're duct-taping systems together, drowning in logins, and wasting hours troubleshooting integrations that never quite work the way they should.

If this sounds familiar, you're not alone. Many service businesses reach a point where their marketing tech stack becomes a barrier to growth rather than a catalyst for it. The solution? Streamlining, or rather, intentionally refining your technology so it becomes a powerful, seamless engine for scaling your brand.

1. Chaos Kills Clarity

One of the greatest costs of an overcomplicated marketing tech stack isn't money - it's clarity. When you have too many tools doing overlapping tasks, it becomes impossible to get a clear, accurate picture of what's working and what isn't.

Consider this possible scenario:

- Your email platform is tracking one set of engagement metrics.
- Your CRM has another set of data on leads and conversions.
- Your ad platform is reporting yet another version of events.

This kind of fragmentation in analytics leads to "data silos," where information lives in disconnected systems that don't talk to each other. Decisions that are not data-driven are for amateurs - and you're in the big leagues now.

Streamlining solves this by aggregating your data, so your tools are integrated or reduced to a single source of truth. You gain:

- Straightforward insights into what's driving revenue.
- Faster decision-making based on real-time data.
- Elimination of duplicate reporting, saving time and reducing errors.

Clarity isn't just a "nice to have", it's a competitive advantage that you quite literally can't afford to do without. Businesses that can quickly interpret accurate data will always outpace those still sorting through clutter…if they are even sorting through it at all.

2. Reducing Costs and Wasted Resources

Every tool in your stack costs you something—whether it's literal direct costs or the hidden cost of team members spending hours learning, maintaining, or troubleshooting it—the tab is running.

Many businesses are shocked when they audit their tech stack and discover how much they're spending on redundant or underused platforms. For example:

- A social media scheduling tool and a CRM with built-in scheduling capabilities.
- A premium analytics tool that no one on the team fully understands, so the features are not being maximized.

One of your key objectives with your marketing tech stack should be:

- Choosing fewer, more powerful tools that can do multiple things well.
- Making strategic investments in platforms that will grow with your business and position you to scale.
- Reclaiming wasted hours spent switching between platforms or fixing broken integrations.

The result is a lean, cost-effective tech stack that supports revenue growth rather than quietly draining profit margins.

3. Enabling Scalability

At a certain stage of business, the goal is to scale—or at least it should be. Scaling a business on a shaky foundation is like building a skyscraper on sand. It doesn't matter how tall you go; eventually, it will collapse. A scattered tech stack creates bottlenecks that make growth impossible and ultimately leads to falling through the cracks because systems aren't syncing properly. The byproduct results in sales and marketing being perpetually misaligned due to inconsistent data.

When you streamline, you design your stack for scalability, ensuring your tools will all work together seamlessly to create a smooth customer experience and give your team the capacity to handle more clients without burning out.

4. Protecting the Client Experience

Your tech stack has a direct impact on how clients experience your brand. Gaps in the client experience make your brand appear ill-prepared and unprofessional, and it will cause serious slippage in the trust tree. Automated, personalized emails and a smooth onboarding process from day one solidifies confidence that they have made the right decision.

When tools are disjointed, clients feel it through:
- Delayed follow-ups after discovery calls.
- Confusing onboarding processes with duplicate forms or missing information.
- Inconsistent messaging across platforms.
- Unclear communication between marketing, sales, and service teams.

When your technology runs smoothly, your clients never have to think about it; they just experience excellence and become automatic ambassadors for your brand.

5. Making Room for Innovation

Through thoughtful streamlining and innovation in how you approach doing business, you free up bandwidth so everyone can thrive in their zone of genius. Innovation requires a stable foundation, and when you can accomplish innovation in your systems, you experience freedom to experiment without chaos.

This creates space for:

- Testing bold new marketing strategies without fear of breaking fragile integrations.
- Adopting cutting-edge tools when they truly add value
- Focusing on high-level creative and strategic work instead of firefighting technical issues.

Where do you begin?

Audit Everything:
- Make a list of every tool currently in use.
- Include costs, usage frequency, and which team members rely on it.

Identify Redundancies:
- Highlight tools that overlap in functionality.
- Decide which one best fits your long-term strategy.

Clarify Core Needs:

- Map out the essential functions your marketing must have:
    - Lead generation
    - Nurturing and automation
    - Conversion tracking
    - Reporting and analytics

Anything outside of these essentials should be evaluated carefully—the goal here is to simplify, not complicate.

Choose Scalable Platforms:

- Look for tools that integrate easily with others and will grow with your business.

Create a Migration Plan:

- Consolidate systems one step at a time to avoid disruption.
- Train your team thoroughly before phasing out old tools.

Document Processes:

- Build SOPs (standard operating procedures) to keep your tech stack streamlined as you grow.

Campaign Development

"Your goal should be to design a digital marketing presence that is purposeful, planned, positioned, and profitable."

~ *Tisha Holman*

This section is based on the method that can be found in The Digital Day Planner I created during the pandemic. When I would speak at conferences or lead workshops, I would always tell the people in the room that the only way being consistent online doesn't become a point of frustration and a monkey on your back is to create editorial and content calendars, then schedule the content so you are free to focus on the areas of your business that really bring in the big bucks. What I didn't specify was how this would be accomplished? Would it be an Excel Spreadsheet or a Microsoft Word document? Where would this be documented? Enter The Digital Day Planner! I call myself an analog girl living in a digital world, and I still love when pen meets paper. The Digital Day Planner is a physical planner and the premier option for planning all of your digital content.

Content Pillars

Content pillars are what help you fill in your editorial and content calendars. Establishing content pillars helps facilitate content that connects and allows you to work smarter, as opposed to harder. Once upon a time, I would encourage small business owners to post daily on all platforms—times have changed! These days, the frequency that you need to post online is more about quantity than quality, but it is still helpful to have a healthy schedule of content, as you want people to come to your channels and be able to jump down a rabbit hole full of your expertise. It will be easier to accomplish if you can make your content make sense across multiple platforms.

What Is A Campaign?

A marketing campaign is an intentional sequence of content and touchpoints, strategically planned and executed across platforms, to drive a measurable outcome.

Campaigns aren't just a collection of random posts; they are a cohesive story that is told across multiple digital platforms with aligned messaging, compelling visuals, and provocative calls to action. Building your content calendar around campaigns keeps you organized by allowing you to plan, fosters consistency, and makes measuring success more practical.

Run The Play!

Allow me to give you some examples of campaigns to help get you started as you make the shift to this new way of developing your content.

TYPES OF CAMPAIGNS

VISIBILITY CAMPAIGNS
Grow reach, build brand awareness, and attract new followers

ENGAGEMENT CAMPAIGNS
Deepen connection with your audience and build the trust tree.

CONVERSION CAMPAIGNS
Drive a specific action like a purchase, event registration, or discovery call.

RETENTION CAMPAIGNS
Nurture existing clients and encourage repeat business and referrals.

1. **Visibility Campaigns** - Grow reach, build brand awareness, and attract new followers.

2. **Engagement Campaigns** - Deepen connection with your audience and build the trust tree.

3. **Conversion Campaigns** - Drive a specific action like a purchase, event registration, or discovery call.

4. **Retention Campaigns** - Nurture existing clients and encourage repeat business and referrals.

How you structure these campaigns is kind of what makes it a campaign.

Use these elements as a guideline:

- Campaign Name
- Campaign Goal
- Start/End Dates
- Main Call to Action
- Platforms
- Key Messages
- Content Plan (types of content)
- How you'll measure success

Use the campaigns as a foundation to fill up your content calendar, tell a great story, and make sure the content connects so it can convert to cash. Get ready to reap the benefits of proactive marketing strategies!

Content pillars are the strategic categories of conversation that align your content with your audience's needs and your business's growth goals. They transform content from random posts into a cohesive system that builds authority, trust, and revenue. Content pillars are deliberate categories of "conversation" in the digital space that will reinforce and solidify your value, attract your Perfect MATCH™, and drive them toward a buying decision. Don't fall into the trap of creating content that satisfies what you think is enough to "sell" what you're selling. Ego sharing doesn't convert to cash—stay client-centric.

When you use pillars:

- Clarity: Your audience always knows what to expect from you.
- Efficiency: Content planning becomes faster and more organized.
- Authority: You consistently show up as the expert in defined areas.
- Conversion: Each piece of content moves people toward a strategic

outcome.

Your editorial calendar should line up with your master calendar. Knowing what is coming up helps you plan content campaigns that are both thoughtful and intentional. Assign them to specific days or weeks and build your content that connects around that. Although one of the benefits of great content pillars is the predictability of what they include, always seek innovation and new, impactful ways to connect with your audience.

Diagram

Content that connects - Video (live, webinar, speaking gig, interview - podcasts) > clips (reels/video) > Blog > newsletter > Memes/carousels > lead magnets

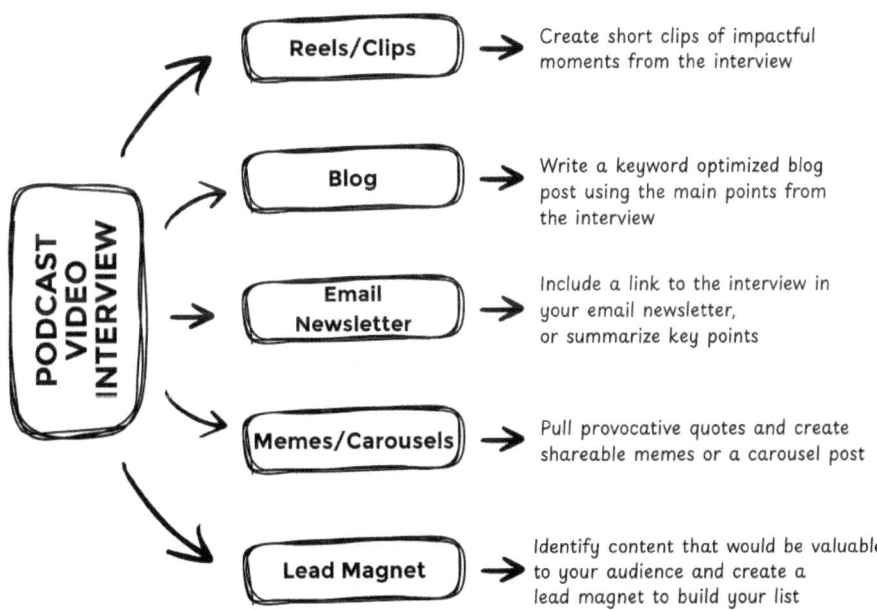

The Digital Day Planner

Use this framework from the pages of The Digital Day Planner to plan for, what I like to call— Good Digital Days.

The Brainstorm - This is where you do the proverbial brain dump and just get all of your ideas out for potential content for the month

Ideate | Innovate | Create - You have your content pillars and general focus in mind - now explore how you can do something innovative or creative that will set you apart from the competition.

Buzzworthy Messaging- This is where you make note of any key phrases, messages, or elements of the CopySignature™ that you want to include.

Goals That Position You to S.C.A.L.E. - Our goals are more than just SMART; they position us to SCALE, set a few for the month so you have something to work towards.

The Email Plan - Create your email subject lines for the month. Choose two for A/B testing and separate them by segment list.

The Blog/Vlog Plan - Decide on your blog or vlog topics for the month.

The Text Plan - Decide on keywords, special offers, and list segments for any text campaigns.

The Podcast Plan - You will likely be further ahead than a month on this one, but decide on those topics, and ensure you have guest details and show descriptions.

The Graphics/Creative Plan - Plan your graphic and video needs for the month and get them into production

Content Calendar - This is where you go to each plan and pull the subject line, topic, etc., for that week and plot into your social media calendar for that week.

Hashtags (#) - These have functioned as content aggregators that, simply put, allowed your content to be seen by larger audiences. Advancements in AI are making them obsolete. Instead of hashtags, lean into buzzworthy messaging to use language that is AI-Engine Optimized (AEO) will maximize searchability across social platforms and search engines.

Content that Converts to Cash - Identify the content with specific calls to action that are tied to financial outcomes. Be sure you are monitoring this content and there are no broken elements in your sales funnels.

Wins/Opportunities - A data-driven strategy is mission-critical to your success online. Review the performance of your content for the week and call out the wins and opportunities so you know where to make adjustments for the next batch of content.

Paid Media - If you are at a point where you are running ads, be sure you are monitoring the performance so you can adjust your ad spend or other multi-variate testing (hooks, captions, visuals) as needed.

This method of content planning is tried, true, and intended to simplify the process for you and your team. Give it a shot and watch how it relieves some of the angst around content creation.

Content That Converts To Cash

**"If your content doesn't have a ROI,
it is a WOT {Waste of Time}!"**

~Tisha Holman

I referenced content that converts to cash in the previous chapter, and I want to add a bit more color to the concept. The content you post won't convert to cash if you don't bring potential clients into your ecosystem and get their information so you can deepen your marketing efforts and move them along in the buying journey.

Story time.

I remember the first time Facebook had a major outage and the entire app shut down for the whole day - and when I say shut down, I mean SHUT DOWN. I can recall repeatedly refreshing my phone, trying to see why the most recent posts were from the day before. It was so bizarre, like a "Left Behind" moment!

The other social media platforms didn't have "stories" and that type of ephemeral content, so folks were pretty much in the dark until Facebook was back online. Once it was restored, there was a litany of posts from small business owners and entrepreneurs complaining about the fact that they were unable to conduct business the entire day and consequently lost money—whose fault was that?

Many small businesses were using Facebook—a platform over which you have no control and no ownership of your followers' information—as their website. So, when the lights went out on Facebook, they too were closed for business and couldn't communicate with their customers or generate any income.

You have to pull followers into your ecosystem so you can collect their information, so an outage on social media doesn't put a hitch in your giddy-up and create a profitability bottleneck in your business operations. This is why I put so much emphasis on the fallacy of vanity metrics. Who cares how many followers or video views you have if the only place you have access to them is in a place you don't own the data. Mind your business!

Before your content can convert, there has to be a call to action. Think about an intersection. If a red light doesn't give a call to action to stop, cars will just keep going with no order or direction…and then crash. Effective calls to action need to compel them to take decisive action with no reservation. A good lead magnet leads them to self-select into exploring how you provide the salve that will solve their most pressing problem in life and business.

Quality / Quantity

It is not about the quantity of content you pump onto your digital platforms; it's the quality. Your content should be irresistible, juicy and tasty like R.I.B.S.

Relevant

Informative

Branded

Shareable

When your content is tasty like R.I.B.S., you create a perpetual flow of opportunities and new brand ambassadors online.

Uncover your P.O.T. of Gold to reveal additional streams of revenue in your business.

P -Products: Your Signature Offers & Scalable Digital Assets

This is the foundation of your revenue engine. Products are the tangible, teachable, repeatable expressions of your expertise. They represent what you do best and how you help people in a structured, results-driven way.

Your products include:

1. Signature Programs and High-Ticket Offers

These are your anchor offers—the ones rooted in your frameworks, methodology, and unique intellectual property-your secret sauce. They typically deliver deeper transformation and higher client engagement.

2. Ancillary Offers and Upsells

These are the complementary solutions your audience needs before, during, or after your signature experience. Think: intensives, VIP days, templates, audits, bootcamps, or micro-trainings. These allow you to serve the same audience at different entry points and investment levels.

3. Self-Guided Courses and Digital Content

This is where you package your expertise into scalable assets that create passive income without diluting your brand. Your digital assets can include online courses, workshops, guides, quizzes, assessments, templates, swipe files, and curriculum bundles.

When your products are aligned and meet the evolving needs of your audience, they create lifelong customers.

O - Opportunities: Visibility Channels That Expand Your Authority and Attract Revenue

Your opportunities represent how your expertise travels. These visibility pipelines expose you to new audiences, strengthen your credibility, and act as entry points for future clients.

Your Opportunities Include:

1. Public Relations and Media Exposure

Press placements validate your expertise through trusted third parties. They expand your reach beyond your existing audience, strengthen brand credibility, and often lead to speaking invitations, partnerships, and higher-caliber clients.

2. Speaking Engagements

When you step on stages—virtual or in person—you accelerate trust. Speaking creates instant intimacy, positions you as a category authority, and drives high-quality leads into your ecosystem.

3. Print & Editorial Features

Magazines, journals, industry publications, and local or national newspapers place your thought leadership directly in front of the audiences that matter. These are evergreen assets that continue to elevate your brand long after they're published.

Opportunities create opportunities to expand your reach and increase demand.

T -Treasures: Intellectual Property That Lives Beyond You

Your treasures are the legacy assets—your most meaningful, long-term, and high-impact expressions of expertise. These are the pieces of content that position you as a thought leader at scale.

Your treasures include:

1. Books

Books open doors, deepen trust, and establish you as a credible voice in your field. A book becomes a revenue stream, a lead generator, a speaking tool, and a lasting demonstration of your intellectual property.

2. Workbooks, Manuals, Guides

These assets support your programs, deepen your methodology, and can be licensed for corporate training, schools, nonprofits, and professional organizations.

3. Frameworks & Models

Your branded frameworks—like STAGE™, CopySignature™, C.O.R.E.™, and Perfect MATCH™—are treasures because they can be expanded, licensed, scaled, and repurposed into countless assets.

Treasures outlive launches and position you as a more just a service provider.

Your POT of Gold is not just another cute acronym in my arsenal. When you leverage all three intentionally, you expand your revenue and reach simultaneously. Cha-Ching!!

Community Building

"Online communities grow when people can see themselves connected to your mission."

~Tisha Holman

A brand in demand is built on connection, trust, and the demonstration of the transformation you provide. Building an online community is how you accomplish that. Facebook used to be the default for Groups. It was free and easy to set up, but the problem of overcoming the algorithm and content being distributed in the group members' timelines has made the juice not worth the squeeze, and then of course, the issue of ownership.

Bring your audience to a space where you have the greatest control of the dynamics of the interactions and provide a VIP experience—this is how you will differentiate yourself and create raving fans. Why be a Facebook group when you can curate an environment that keeps them coming back for more?

To keep this playbook as evergreen as possible, I won't get too deep in the weeds on specific online community alternatives other than Facebook—but here are the reasons why you need to make the move to a space in which you own and can control the user experience.

1. Owning your community means owning your data and your voice. You own the data and you control the user experience. That ownership gives you the freedom to design a community that evolves with the growth of your brand.

2. Turn down the noise. Independent platforms allow you to start meaningful conversations and manage notifications in a structured way. Subscription models that create opportunities for exclusive access are another way you can create content that converts to cash.

3. Monetization beyond the ads. Many independent platforms can host live events, courses, and more right inside of your community. You'll be able to generate income directly from inside the community rather than treating it like a lead-generation tool.

4. A BRANDED Experience. Elevate your brand through customized layouts, use of your branding and color schemes - some even have mobile apps, making the experience even more convenient and valuable to your audience.

5. Real Transformation. One of the most beautiful aspects of building your own online community is that you have the ability to create a hub

for focused learning environments that turn into real results for your clients.

Just as you would with other elements of the CORE Model, create a plan for engagements in this space. If by chance you still have a Facebook community, create a migration plan that makes the move to the new territory seamless for your community members.

You'll soon see that there are so many possibilities for how you can build your online community. A word to the wise: Don't try to keep up with the Joneses. Challenge yourself to innovate and set yourself clearly apart from your competition but do only what you and your team can keep up with.

Ethical AI

"Don't allow technology to remove the heartbeat from the voice of your brand."
~*Tisha Holman*

AI is here to STAY. I could end the chapter right here and let you move on to the next section, but I'll stay and say a little more - strong emphasis on little. Why, you ask? Because AI is growing at such a rapid rate, going into any significant details would make this content irrelevant by the time this book goes to print. What I am going to briefly explore is the concept of ethical AI, because no matter how rapidly the technology evolves, this is a principle that should always guide your use of the tool as a responsible small business owner.

Let's get technical for a second. If you are going to use the tool in your business, let's get to know the technology.

Machine Learning - A subfield of artificial intelligence that gives computers the ability to identify patterns and learn from data without explicitly being programmed.

Natural Language Processing - A type of AI that allows computers to speak and understand human language.

These two, amongst other things, are working in tandem behind the scenes to make AI seem like less of the A and more of the I. I wanted you to have some familiarity with these terms, as they are at a high level and what essentially works in the background to "train" your AI tools to "think" like your brand and "speak" in your voice. Like any tool, the impact it has will depend on how you use it.

So, the million-dollar question, figuratively and quite possibly literally, is: How can you use it to integrate systems and increase productivity? AI can provide you with robust, smarter insights, and data-driven strategies that can make your navigation through the CORE Model even more fruitful.

When leveraged ethically and strategically, AI can free up bandwidth, streamline operations, and position you to scale faster. When used irresponsibly, it will dilute the brand voice you are working so hard to develop, push your audience out of the trust tree, and possibly expose you to legal consequences and repercussions.

You are here because you are, or aspire to be, a high-achieving small business owner building a business that is purposeful and profitable - right? Right. So, get more sophisticated and strategic in your use of AI and leave the ranks of those writing eBooks, creating glamour shots, and "hard truth"-ing us to death in their social media copy. If you know what I mean, you know what I mean. Predictive analytics can help identify which types of content are likely to perform best, based on historical data and audience behavior, and predict industry trends. You can leverage sentiment analysis, better known as social listening, to put your ear to the ground of those digital highways and byways to analyze how your followers feel, and what the narrative is about your products/services/events - can you imagine how valuable that could be to you and your business?

AI isn't coming for your potential customers; it is exposing your gaps and inefficiencies. Hard truth (it's ok to laugh here).

It may seem obvious, but I am going to say this anyway. Let's talk about a few areas where Ethical AI matters most:

1. **Transparency** - The trust tree can't be a "Charlie Brown" tree. Don't let your use of AI impact your credibility as an expert. Your clients and audience deserve to know when they are being served AI-generated content and concepts.

2. **Privacy and Data Protection** - The rapid and widespread adoption of AI necessitates feeding it the data it needs to function properly. I may be dating myself with this one, but do you remember the movie, Little Shop of Horrors? "Feed me, Seymour!" If you are feeding it sensitive customer information, take caution because you really can't account for how that information is being used.

3. **Human and Heart** - AI can help you scale, but it can't replace what you have in lived experience, intuition, and expertise. AI tools are fantastic, but don't allow them to become the pulse of your brand.

Use AI to connect the dots, not create them! Strike a careful balance between innovation and intention.

- Automate repetitive administrative tasks
- Enhance your client onboarding experience
- Streamline marketing operations

SIDELINE SIGNAL!

A great place to explore innovation is through the possibilities of Agentic AI. I'm not just talking about after-hours canned messages and FAQs. Dig deeper and differentiate.

I mentioned that AI can help you amplify strategy, analytics, and optimization! I've created a list of prompts that will get you started on this journey. Try them out!

1. Audience Insights:

Prompt: "Analyze customer behavior data for [YOUR BUSINESS] to identify trends in purchasing habits, preferred communication channels, and peak engagement times."

Business Benefit: Strategic understanding of audience preferences.

2. Content Performance Review:

Prompt: "Evaluate the past 3 months of Instagram and LinkedIn posts for [YOUR BUSINESS]. Identify which types of posts (e.g., videos, carousel posts, stories) generated the most engagement and why."

Business Benefit: Data-driven content planning.

3. Competitor Benchmarking:

Prompt: "Analyze [specific competitor's] social media strategy. What are their top-performing posts, engagement tactics, and areas for improvement compared to [YOUR BUSINESS]?"

Business Benefit: Competitive edge through targeted improvements.

SIDE NOTE: This is the only instance I suggest peeping the competition...so you can see what they are doing and blaze a trail around them.

4. SEO Keyword Gap Analysis:

Prompt: "Identify keyword opportunities that [YOUR BUSINESS] is not targeting but competitors are ranking for in [specific industry]."

Business Benefit: Improved organic traffic through refined keyword strategy.

5. Audience Segmentation:

Prompt: "Based on CRM data for [YOUR BUSINESS], segment customers into groups based on behavior, demographics, and purchasing patterns. Suggest tailored marketing strategies for each group."

Business Benefit: Targeted and personalized marketing strategies and tactics.

6. Email Campaign Insights:

Prompt: "Review the last 6 months of email campaign performance for [YOUR BUSINESS]. Highlight the most effective subject lines, CTAs, and send times to improve future campaigns."

Business Benefit: Increased open rates and conversion rates.

7. Ad Spend Optimization:

Prompt: "Analyze the ROI of recent Google Ads and Facebook Ads campaigns for [YOUR BUSINESS]. Identify which campaigns delivered the highest ROI and suggest adjustments to underperforming ones."

Business Benefit: Increased ROI from paid advertising efforts.

8. Website Traffic Patterns:

Prompt: "Analyze traffic data for [your website]. Identify the most visited pages, the top sources of referral traffic, and areas with high bounce rates."

Business Benefit: Optimized website and user experience.

9. Social Listening Insights:

Prompt: "Use AI tools to monitor social media mentions of [your business or industry keyword]. Highlight trends in audience sentiment and commonly asked questions."

Business Benefit: Real-time understanding of brand sentiment, content prompt harvesting.

10. Sales Funnel Insights:

Prompt: "Examine the conversion rates at each stage of [YOUR BUSINESS] sales funnel. Recommend improvements for the stages with the most significant drop-offs."

Business Benefit: Better sales performance, targeted funnel optimization.

Unlikely Mentors:
Duke Ellington
Reach Scaled Through Systems &
Consistency

Duke Ellington was an influencer before his time. Ellington revolutionized Harlem through his creation of new experiences and distribution channels that expanded his reach far beyond any one musical performance.

So, what did he do?

⇒ Secured a residency at the Cotton Club, giving him consistent visibility in front of the right audience.

⇒ Leveraged radio, the "social media" of the era, to broadcast performances nationally.

⇒ Created a polished, reliable brand experience through his orchestra, making every performance a signature event.

Lesson for Reach:

Leverage platforms, partnerships, and repeatable processes to expand visibility consistently. In the day-to-day operations of your business, this is how you build reach across multiple digital platforms that don't depend solely on you showing up live every day.

Questions:

- Which of your current marketing channels feels like a Cotton Club residency, giving you consistent, predictable reach?
- Where are you still depending on hustle instead of structure to grow your audience?
- If you stopped showing up tomorrow, would your reach continue to grow, or would that be the final act?

Section Summary: Revenue/Reach

Run The Play!

1. Create a Revenue Map: List every current revenue stream, including average monthly revenue, effort required, and scalability potential.

2. Define a Flagship Offer: Identify or refine one core offer that will become the centerpiece of your revenue strategy.

3. Establish Reach Channels: Determine where your audience is most active and choose 2 primary platforms to dominate.

Prompts

- What percentage of your marketing effort is focused on acquisition vs. retention?

- Which offers are generating the most revenue but draining your energy the most?

- How can you expand your reach without spreading yourself thin?

Execution

EXECUTION

"A plan without execution is just potential waiting for permission."

~Tisha Holman

E xecution is where strong businesses come to profit and scale. When your business executes consistently:

⇒ Your audience starts to trust your brand (because it's consistent)

⇒ Your team starts to anticipate and lead (because they have clarity).

⇒ Your offers become more refined (because you're iterating and optimizing).

⇒ You regain time, energy, and creative bandwidth (because systems run the show).

Doesn't this sound exciting? Can you visualize your company running in this manner? Mindset matters - start thinking and executing like the CEO you are destined to be.

What Keeps Founders From Executing

Can you see yourself in any of these pitfalls of great progress?

- Perfectionism: "I'm still working on it." (But it has been weeks, and you just want to go through again and make sure everything is perfect before you share it with the world. Analysis paralysis is a real thing, and I have been here many times myself.

- Overwhelm: Too many priorities = no progress on any of them. (It might be time to grow that team.)

- Lack of clarity: You don't know what the next right move is because you hadn't planned this far ahead, and now you don't know which way to go.

- No accountability: No one is checking your progress... not even you. (Yikes.)

- Disorganized systems: You don't know where anything lives or how to find it. (SOPs and documentation of your systems will be your life raft here.

Why Execution Is Your Leverage Point

We've all seen it.

- The incredible idea that never gets launched.
- The marketing plan that dies in a Google Doc.
- The client experience that never gets optimized because no one "has time."
- The team that's busy... but not productive.
- The goals that feel exciting in January and are forgotten by March.

This part of the C.O.R.E.™ Model is about creating a rhythm that keeps the important things moving forward without you doing the same tasks a different way each time. That is exhausting.

Execution is the step where many small businesses stall. It's not because they don't have the drive; it's more so because they don't have the proper structure in place. The goals are big and the potential is there; however, without a disciplined engine of implementation, everything sits on the digital shelf labeled "someday."

This is where the final piece of the C.O.R.E.™ Model. Execution—steps in to change the game, or at least keep you in the game.

Execution is the engine of the C.O.R.E.™ model. The Execution phase is the magical place where your strategy, operations, and plan for monetization come together to create a system that keeps your business not just moving, but moving consistently. Repeatable processes that make success predictable are coming your way.

Execution ≠ Hustle

Execution in the C.O.R.E.™ system is strategic, prioritized, system-supported action. It supports you in making measurable progress toward meaningful goals. This is the beautiful intersection where your strategy meets your master calendar, your offers meet your Perfect MATCH™, and strong systems support your daily decisions—no hustle culture here. There is no glamour in burning the candle at both ends and therefore putting the flow of your business—and your health —in jeopardy.

Goals that S.C.A.L.E.

"If your goals aren't built to S.C.A.L.E., they are built to stall."

~*Tisha Holman*

S.M.A.R.T. Goals are great, but it is my belief that high-achieving small business owners need to set different types of goals when it comes to how they show up in the digital world—goals that actually move the needle and get them closer to seeing conversion and experiencing sustainable growth. The S.C.A.L.E. framework guides you towards setting goals that are not only aligned with your strategy, but are also intentionally designed to generate profits, reinforce your place as an expert and thought leader, and expand your reach online.

Strategy-Aligned: Supports the strategic plan and goals you have developed

Client-Centric: Every action is designed with your Perfect M.A.T.C.H.™ in mind

Actionable & Automated: Your systems keep things moving like a well-oiled machine

Leveraged across channels: Content that connects to cash on every platform

Expert- Reinforcing: Positions you as an expert and thought-leader in your industry

Strategy-Aligned

Your goals don't exist in a vacuum, and they need to directly support your overarching business and marketing strategy. Keeping your goals strategically aligned keeps you from falling into the trap of social comparison and on track with accomplishing the goals and objectives you have set for your business.

TIME OUT!

Let's park here for a moment and talk about social comparison. This is something that you have to be very mindful of as it pertains to your "competitors". Imposter syndrome is the underbelly of this beast, and the slope is slippery. Remember, you are only interested in what others are doing to the extent of market research, and what others do in the digital space does not drive or shift your strategy. This is where those strategic anchors that we learned about in the Revenue & Reach section of the model become very important.

Examples of Strategy-Aligned Goals:

- Launching a new offer that fills a gap in your brand's ecosystem.

- Creating a 90-day lead generation campaign that aligns with your sales goals for that quarter.

- Creating a campaign and funnel that supports one of your offers or programs.

Client-Centric

Serving the needs, interests, and pain points that mark the transformational journey of your Perfect M.A.T.C.H.™ should be your primary focus. Although I believe wholeheartedly that we should share our wins publicly to not only celebrate ourselves, but also to allow others to celebrate with us, your goals for your content should build connection and community with your audience. I have helped so many small business owners re-focus their content strategy in this area—keep your clients at the forefront of everything you share online.

Examples of Client-Centric Goals:

- Designing a lead magnet that speaks directly to a specific pain point your Perfect M.A.T.C.H™ has.

- Creating social media content that clearly demonstrates the transformational results the client will experience through partnering with you to help them self-select into your offer.

- Streamlining your client onboarding processes to create a better, more enriched experience.

Actionable & Automated

Great goals get executed, and for you, that means turning them into repeatable systems and processes that don't require you to grind. Remember, gears only grind when they are out of alignment, and to continue to move forward causes damage–sometimes the irreparable kind. The digital space can be both a lonely & a noisy place, and you simply cannot scale chaos.

Examples of Actionable & Automated Goals

- Turning high-performing content into evergreen content campaigns
- Automating lead intake and nurture sequences
- Creating SOPs for new processes and procedures

Leveraged Across Channels

Anything that you post on one platform has a place on all of your platforms. Building your campaigns intentionally with content that connects will be your secret weapon for growth online. Don't make this harder than it needs to be. Create multiple opportunities for potential clients to encounter your content to reinforce magnetic messaging- and make sure it is testable, scalable, and practical.

Examples of Leveraged Goals

- A launch that has a layered impact
- A strategic partnership with an influencer that has a similar Perfect MATCH audience
- Repurposing impactful content that performed well to grow your audience

Expert-Reinforcing

Your goals should support your regular demonstration showing yourself to be the top expert and thought leader in your industry. Visibility without credibility doesn't convert. Strong thought-leadership, expertise, and social proof of amazing transformational results are the things that keep you top of mind for referrals. It is not enough for you to show up online; you must also clearly differentiate yourself from your competitors.

Example of Expert-Reinforcing Goals
- Posting strong clips from a speaking gig
- Celebrate wins that magnify your brilliance - awards, recognition, etc.
- Canonize your thought-leadership by writing a book

Let me give you an example:

Goal: Launch a signature lead magnet to grow my email list by 500 Perfect M.A.T.C.H.™ subscribers over a 45-day period and position myself as the go-to expert digital strategist. I want to automate this nurture sequence and also repurpose content on LinkedIn, YouTube, and Instagram.

Strategy-Aligned —This goal directly supports the overall strategy to increase lead flow, expand visibility, and nurture a warm audience for an upcoming launch of The Digital Marketing Kickstart™.

Client Centric — Create a lead magnet that speaks directly to my Perfect M.A.T.C.H.™ that is struggling with content that does not convert to cash. It solves a real point while naturally leading into my offer.

Actionable & Automated — The lead magnet is created, branded, and loaded in my Customer Relationship Management tool, with logic set up for an automated 3-part email welcome sequence that nurtures the lead toward booking a Let's Talk Session with me. The Standard Operating Procedures for the development of the lead magnet, graphics, copy for social media, and scheduling in my social media scheduling tool are documented so my team can manage the process moving forward

Leveraged across channels —The lead magnet is repurposed into Content That Connects:

A YouTube video explaining the strategy

A LinkedIn newsletter breaking down the concept

A carousel post on Instagram introducing the lead magnet

Stories, DM's and Reels to drive traffic back to the download for the
lead magnet

Expert-Reinforcing— The lead magnet is created as a goal-ready to SCALE, and it uses the Mind Your Business CopySignature™, which naturally reinforces my unique thought leadership in my industry. I'm not tossing around fluff; I am showcasing this brilliant proprietary process designed to help them create a digital marketing presence that is planned, positioned, purposeful, and profitable.

BOOM! (Which GIF came to mind when I said that? For me, it's the dinner table scene from Tyler Perry's Why Did I Get Married. IYKYK)

The Ultimate System

"Systems make success predictable. There should not be one thing you are doing as a business owner that is random, haphazard, or not tied to a measurable result."
~*Tisha Holman*

The systems in your business need to be repeatable and replicable, as that will be how you operate efficiently behind the scenes. Systems yield a predictable flow of clients, which for you, equates to repeatable business and frees up your time. Well-designed systems will not only help you attract your Perfect MATCH, but the attraction will also feel organized for you and them. Don't be a flash in the pan that hits success and then can't repeat it.

Setting the STAGE for Success

I have distilled the ULTIMATE system you can use to keep your business on a trajectory to that planned, positioned, purposeful, and profitable online presence. I call it the S.T.A.G.E.™ System because you're not just showing up online, you are owning the stage you have strategically set and driving results like the star you are.

S - Strategy First

T – Tactical Planning

A – Asset Creation & Content Production

G – Growth & Distribution Systems

E – Evaluate & Elevate

Strategy First —The foundation and blueprint for all marketing activities.

We have already talked a lot about strategy. You know that it's the difference between a business that shows up online with purpose and clarity, and one that's constantly reacting to trends, algorithms, and competitor moves. Without a strategy, you may be busy — even visible — but you won't be effective long term. This first stage of the S.T.A.G.E.™ System is where you define who you are, what you stand for, and how you'll connect with the people you're meant to serve.

This is why the Clarity phase of the CORE Model is so important. It positions you to knock it out of the park in the other phases.

The Pillars of a Strong Marketing Strategy

At this stage, your focus should be on establishing the core elements that will direct your digital marketing efforts. As a refresher, these are the pillars that everything else will rest on:

1. Brand Clarity

Your brand is more than a logo or tagline. It's the promise you make to your audience and the experience they can expect when they interact with you. When you have brand clarity, you avoid one of the biggest traps in digital marketing: blending into the noise. Your clarity gives you the confidence to take a stand, communicate boldly, and attract the clients who are aligned with the transformation you provide.

2. Audience Definition (Perfect M.A.T.C.H.™)

The most powerful marketing strategies are built around deep audience understanding. Your goal isn't just to reach "people," but to connect with your Perfect M.A.T.C.H.™ clients — the ones who are magnetized to your message, aligned with your values, and ready to take action. This clarity ensures that every marketing effort is targeted and resonates deeply with the right audience.

3. Positioning and Messaging (CopySignature™)

Once you know who you serve, you must clearly communicate why you are the best answer to the problem they need to solve. Your CopySignature™ is your brand's unique messaging DNA. When your positioning is solid, you no longer compete on price or features. Instead, you occupy a distinct space in your client's mind — one that competitors can't easily replicate because it's your secret sauce.

4. Clear Business Objectives

Finally, no strategy is complete without defining measurable outcomes- we have to know what success looks like for ourselves, right? Without clear objectives, you are wasting your time because the tasks you are working on aren't working toward anything specific.

Common Mistakes at the Strategy Stage

Skipping this stage or rushing through it leads to predictable problems later:

- Random acts of marketing: Scattered campaigns with no cohesion or consistency.

- Shifty messaging: A brand voice that shifts across platforms, confusing your audience.

- Wasted resources: Investing in ads prematurely, purchasing tools that don't support your goals, and campaigns that don't align with actual business goals.

- Missing targets: Attracting followers who don't convert into clients.

Run The Play!

Creating Your Strategy Blueprint

Here's how to get started:

1. Clarify Your Brand Promise:
    Write one clear statement that describes who you serve, the transformation you create, and how you deliver it.

2. Define Your Perfect M.A.T.C.H.™ Audience:
    Create a profile of your ideal client using the five key alignment indicators.

3. Develop Your CopySignature™:
    Identify the core phrases, tone, and messaging pillars that will guide all communication.

4. Set Measurable Objectives:
    Choose 3–5 specific, revenue-aligned goals for the next 90 days.

5. Document Your Strategy:
    Put everything into a one-page strategy summary that can guide your team and partners.

Strategy isn't glamorous. It happens behind the scenes, away from the spotlight. But it's what separates brands that constantly hustle for relevance from those that lead their markets with clarity and confidence.

By investing deeply in this stage, you create a foundation that not only supports your current marketing but also scales seamlessly as your business grows. In other words, you don't just get ready for the next campaign — you get ready to own the stage.

Tactical Planning — Translating strategy into a step-by-step execution plan.

Once you've built a strong digital marketing strategy, the next challenge is putting everything in motion. This is where many businesses stumble. They have a clear vision and well-defined goals, but without a tactical plan, they end up reacting to problems instead of driving results.

Tactical planning is the bridge between strategy and action. It's where you take big-picture ideas and break them down into specific steps, timelines, and responsibilities. Without this step, even the most brilliant strategy will remain a good idea that never came to fruition. Tactical planning eliminates guesswork by bringing order and structure to your marketing efforts. It ensures that every task serves a larger purpose and that everyone on your team understands how their role contributes to business growth.

The Core Components of Tactical Planning

To create a plan that drives meaningful results, focus on these four key components:

1. Campaign Mapping

Campaigns are the heartbeat of your digital marketing efforts. Each campaign represents a focused, time-bound effort designed to achieve a specific goal. Campaign mapping gives you a clear view of how each moving part fits together, preventing wasted effort and inconsistent messaging.

2. Resource Allocation

Many businesses struggle here because they underestimate the resources required. Once campaigns are mapped, the next step is identifying who and what is needed to bring them to life:

- People: Assigning roles and responsibilities to team members or contractors.
- Time: Estimating the hours required for each task and scheduling accordingly.
- Budget: Allocating dollars for ads, software, design, and other expenses.

3. Timeline Development

Establishing realistic deadlines is a commitment to deliver results on time and on budget. Due dates and deadlines hold you and your team accountable to the vision.

4. Risk Management

Whether it's a tech issue, delays with a supplier, or a team member suddenly unavailable, stuff happens. The idea here is to be proactive, not reactive. Proactive risk management helps you prepare for the unexpected, so campaigns stay on track. Always have a backup plan for your backup plan.

Common Pitfalls in Tactical Planning

Even experienced teams can hit roadblocks and experience bottlenecks in their work. Watch out for:

- Overcomplication: A plan with too many moving parts can paralyze execution.

- Lack of ownership: Without clear accountability, tasks fall through the cracks.
- Shiny object syndrome: Getting distracted by new tools or tactics that don't align with strategy.
- Ignoring capacity limits: Overloading the team without adjusting timelines or scope.

By anticipating these pitfalls, you can create a plan that is both ambitious and realistic.

Run The Play!

The Digital Day Planner will be your secret weapon—have you ordered your copy?

In the meantime, here's a step-by-step process to get started:

1. Review your strategy: Ensure all campaigns tie directly to your strategic objectives

2. Choose one primary campaign: Focus your team's energy on a single, high-impact initiative before adding more

3. Map the customer journey: Define every stage, from awareness to conversion

4. List required assets: Identify the content, technology, and resources needed.

5. Assign roles and responsibilities: Clarify ownership of each task.

6. Build your timeline: Sequence tasks and set milestone dates.

7. Identify risks: Develop backup plans for critical components.

Asset Creation & Content Production — Building the tools, content, and resources to bring the plan to life.

Digital marketing assets bring your strategic vision to life.

Pause.

Just to make sure we are all on the same page, let me clarify what I mean by assets. Assets, in this instance, are graphics, videos - the visuals that will bring your strategy to life. Assets can also be documents, webpages, data, or anything digitally tangible for your business.

The challenge is not just creating assets, but designing assets that are BRANDED™. Too many just churn out graphics that don't align with their strategy, connect and convert to cash, or support growth—it creates bumps in the client's journey.

The Three Types of Marketing Assets

Not all assets are created equal. Let's dig into three key categories of assets that are the wind beneath your brand's wings.

1. Foundational Assets

These are the non-negotiables - the assets every business needs to operate effectively online. They are your brand's digital infrastructure. Some are public facing; some are for internal use.

Let me give you a few examples:

- Website:

  Your hub for all of your marketing efforts. ALL roads lead to your website. In case you were wondering, YES, you still need a website!

- Brand & Editorial Guides:

  Visual and messaging standards to ensure consistency.

- Lead Capture Systems:

  Automated tools and integrations that put potential clients in your ecosystem.

- Email Marketing Platform: This could also be a part of your CRM tool:

  A system for nurturing clients on the various steps of their journey to working with you.

2. Campaign Assets

Campaign assets are created specifically to support content pillars and then any content that is time-bound.

Examples include:

- Email sequences for a product launch or live event,
- Social media posts for a specific offer

3. Evergreen Assets

Evergreen assets are timeless and will always be of interest and valuable to your audience. They are often repurposed to continuously attract and nurture your Perfect MATCH™. My go-to example is the Bible. For faith-based organizations, the Bible is a constant that is not going to change, and its content will always be valuable to the people following it.

Run The Play!

Batch Content Creation

You are a busy leader, and the time it takes to create the content and assets you need can be significant. What I like to do with my busy clients is plan what I call a Content Development Session. To prepare for this time together, we collaboratively look at their strategy and master calendar to see what content needs to be created to support their work online. Bring multiple options for clothing or create a "uniform" for your brand. As you take pictures and record videos, switch up the clothing, etc., so it looks like you didn't record everything on the same day. Your graphic designers and videographer will take it from there and provide you with all the assets you need to cover the time you planned for, ideally 1-3 months. I know that 3 months sounds overwhelming, start with 1 to get the hang of things and build up to longer runways of time.

Growth & Distribution Systems — Expanding reach, visibility, and audience engagement.

Includes:

Many businesses equate growth with reach. They chase more followers, bigger ad impressions, and higher vanity metrics—and don't realize they are running in place, going nowhere fast. Your true growth isn't just about being seen, you want to be seen by the right folks.

Let's dive into three key areas that you want to consider and focus on growth:

1. Organic Growth: Growing the Trust Tree and Establishing Authority

Organic growth is a long game, especially with all of the many and constant changes in the platforms and algorithms. Organic growth doesn't involve any ads or paid media, and many find themselves discouraged by the lack of movement on their channels. I'll say it again: this is a long game—when people discover your brand online, you want them to be able to fall down a rabbit hole, consuming your content. The growth here might look slow and stagnant—do it anyway.

Key organic growth strategies:

- Content Marketing:

    Create consistent, relevant content that educates, inspires, or solves a problem.

- Search Engine Optimization (SEO):

    Optimize your website and content to attract traffic from search engines. Focus on natural language that aligns with your Perfect M.A.T.C.H.™ audience's needs. Traditionally, SEO has meant using keywords, but advancements in AI have given priority to the content that feels relevant to what they are searching for.

- Community Building:

    Curate bespoke spaces where your audience can connect and grow together.

2. Paid Media: Accelerating Results

Paid ads allow you to target specific audiences and can be very helpful for increasing awareness of your brand, gaining visibility for live events, and positioning your lead magnets to new audiences. The biggest benefit is the ability to be intentional about what groups of people are being served with your content on their timelines and search engines.

Paid media strategies:

- Social Media Ads:

  Use platforms like LinkedIn, YouTube, and Instagram to reach specific segments of your audience.

- Retargeting Campaigns:

  Stay top-of-mind by re-engaging people who've interacted with your brand.

- Paid Partnerships:

  Collaborate with influencers and brands with aligned audiences to expand your reach.

3. Strategic Distribution: Getting More From Every Asset

Distribution is about extending the life and reach of every asset you create. Too many businesses work hard to produce content and campaigns, only to let them fade after a single use.

Strategic distribution ensures you maximize ROI by:

- **Repurposing:** Turn one asset into multiple formats.

  Example: A recorded webinar becomes a YouTube playlist, a podcast episode, a LinkedIn carousel, and a blog post.

- **Cross-Promotion:** Share assets across multiple channels to increase visibility without extra production work.

- **Sequencing:** Plan when and where each piece of content appears to create a steady flow of visibility.

Evaluate & Elevate — Measuring results and optimizing for continual improvement.

This is where being a data-driven brand reenters the chat. If you aren't using the data and analytics to guide your strategic decisions, then you're just guessing…that's not you, right? Great brands are intentional about every aspect of their business, including and especially their digital marketing presence.

Evaluate: Measure and Diagnose

This is simply about measuring what matters. This is not the space for vanity metrics; it is where data-driven decisions are made and success is measured.

Your mileage may vary as you need to determine the key performance indicators that align with your business. Here are a few common metrics that will likely be valuable to you and your team:

1. **Reach:**
   Are you consistently expanding your audience?
   Example KPIs: new followers, website visitors, impressions.
1. **Engagement:**
   Are people having meaningful interactions with your brand?
   Example KPIs: comments, shares, average watch time, click-through rates.
2. **Conversion:**
   Are your marketing efforts turning prospects into paying customers?
   Example KPIs: lead-to-client ratio, sales calls booked, revenue per campaign.
3. **Retention:**
   Are you keeping and nurturing the clients you already have?
   Example KPIs: churn rate, repeat purchases, lifetime value (LTV).

4. **Return on Investment (ROI):**

   Is your marketing spend generating a profit?

   Example KPIs: cost per acquisition (CPA), return on ad spend (ROAS).

I know this can be a lot if you aren't already in the practice of evaluating the numbers. Adapt this workflow to help you navigate being effective in this area:

The Evaluation Workflow:

1. Gather the Data: Pull information about your content from ALL of your digital platforms — social media analytics, email marketing tools, ad dashboards, sales reports, everywhere!

2. Identify Patterns: Look for trends across the various platforms, campaigns, and channels.

3. Diagnose Problems: Determine where the inefficiencies are happening.

4. Highlight Successes: Note which strategies are producing exceptional results and should be repeated, repurposed, and scaled.

 **SIDELINE SIGNAL!**

Schedule monthly reviews for campaigns and quarterly deep dives for overall marketing performance. Consistency is key to staying proactive rather than reactive.

Elevate

Once you have the data, it's time to leverage it to make any tweaks necessary to keep you on a pathway to success. The formula here is very simple, but also mission-critical.

Three Paths to Elevation:
1. Refine: Tweak what's underperforming.
2. Replicate: Scale what's working well
3. Reimagine: Innovate for future growth.

Get into the rhythm of things

How often should I review this information? Keep it simple, keep it consistent—and, of course, do what makes dollars and sense for your brand.

- Weekly Check-Ins: Quick pulse on campaign performance and immediate issues.
- Monthly Reviews: Analyze metrics, adjust tactics, and allocate resources.
- Quarterly Deep Dives: Reassess strategy, messaging, and offers to ensure alignment with business goals.
- Annual Reset: Big-picture review to set direction for the year ahead.

To make sure you keep this in the proper perspective, allow me to share some common pitfalls to look out for as you build this system into your team culture. Avoiding these pitfalls ensures evaluation leads to meaningful growth, not the notorious analysis paralysis.

- Tracking too much data: Measuring everything makes things murky and can overwhelm the team.
- Ignoring context: Facts over feelings all day, but when it comes to digital marketing, numbers alone don't tell the full story; don't forget those qualitative insights.

- Lack of follow-through: Gathering data without taking action wastes everyone's time.

- Waiting too long to review: You don't want to miss the wave of making critical adjustments that can be tougher to course correct later.

SIDELINE SIGNAL!

Success for your business should be predictable because of the systems you have in place. For successful small business owners, execution happens because there's a cadence. Think of this like the heartbeat of your business. Weekly, monthly, quarterly rhythms that turn plans into real results.

Here are a few examples of what that could look like for you:

Rhythm	Purpose	Sample Actions
Weekly CEO Review	Recalibrate tasks & review key metrics	Check lead flow, revenue targets, and team output
Team Meeting	Align projects & remove blockers	Share priorities, flag issues, assign outcomes
Monthly Reset	Analyze progress, profits & adjust goals	Update dashboards, optimize plans leveraging the data
Quarterly Planning	Refocus on big-picture direction	Map launches, content pillars, and continue to fine-tune your systems.

The CEO Role in Execution

If your business can't run without you, you don't own a business; you own a job. You may feel like you're doing alright now financially, and things seem to be going smoothly, but I have to give you a reality check, my friend. You will never scale and truly experience real profits until that business can run like a well-oiled machine without you.

I understand delegating tasks and big responsibilities can be a challenging thing. But remember, you have done your due diligence in the hiring process, so you have to climb a little higher in the trust tree and let your team flourish.

Try this on for size:
- Set the goals and priorities - clarify what matters most this quarter.
- Assign outcomes - not just tasks, but the why behind them.
- Create space for yourself - time block your own creative execution blocks.
- Review & recalibrate - create a 30-minute weekly "CEO check-in" meeting (even if it's just you).

A lot of people tap out at this point. Strategy development feels exciting; curating content lets the creative juices flow; the systems feel like you're building something great—but execution? Execution is hard work! It may feel that way at first - but the reward comes once the groundwork you've laid allows you to step back and be a real boss. Once you see things really start to move in your business, this phase of the CORE Model becomes one of your favorites.

Run The Play!

Identify three core KPIs for each marketing stage: reach, engagement, and conversion.

⇒ Schedule recurring evaluation meetings with your team.

⇒ Audit your current tech stack to ensure you can easily gather accurate data.

⇒ Create an "elevation plan" with specific steps to refine, replicate, and reimagine.

The Power of Continuous Improvement

Evaluate & Elevate is where your digital marketing becomes a living, dynamic system, not a series of random one-off campaigns. It's how you ensure your efforts remain relevant, efficient, and effective — no matter how platforms, audiences, or market conditions change. The Evaluate & Elevate stage is your final step, but it's also your ongoing commitment.

If you can stay the course and find your rhythm here, every strategy, tactic, and asset will continue to propel you to increased profits, exponential growth, and greater impact. The best outcome here, and I must say my personal favorite, is diligence in this area allows your business to stay at the forefront of its industry and command the stage for years to come.

Live Events

"In the right spaces and places, your message becomes an unparalleled, bespoke experience."

~*Tisha Holman*

I used to be an event planner, so when I created the 3E framework, it was through my understanding of what it takes for events to be successful. It was easy for me to connect the logistics of events to how digital marketing could take things to the next level. An executive from an organization that hosts a HUGE annual conference reached out to me because, although the magic was happening in the room, the buzz online was nonexistent. Where they were missing the mark was that the content online was just the obligatory posts giving information about the event. There wasn't anything really speaking to their core audience that would compel them to take action other than to keep scrolling.

From my vantage point, the fix was simple: the strategy for what was happening online needed to align with and complement what was happening in the room.

I was able to create opportunities for live engagement, monetization, and registrations for the conference.

The data and analytics from the event showed a 23% improvement across the board. I don't know what it was about the number 23, but I was happy to see that kind of impact!

You've put in the work to fill the room—but what about everyone watching from the sidelines? Too many small business owners focus only on closing the business in the room, missing out on massive opportunities to expand their reach, engage their audience, and set the stage for future growth.

Your live event is an opportunity to create undeniable brand authority, generate leads, and maximize revenue—but only if you have the right digital strategy in place.

The 3E Formula

Excite — Get the online audience excited about the event. Go beyond the status quo and create a level of FOMO that will keep them glued to your timelines and plan to ensure they are in the room next time. As much as I would love to provide some examples, I am instead going to charge you with finding your way outside of the typical promotion box to discover something unique that pulls your audience into the online conversation.

Engage — Your team should capitalize on this chance to gather evergreen content that can be both used as social proof of the transformation you provided, and for promotion of future events. Grab those testimonials while the energy is high at the event. Create ambassadors for the event and your brand by tapping into the reach of UGC (user-generated content) to keep engagement high. Live events are a content goldmine.

Elevate — We are all kids at heart - who doesn't enjoy a little fun at an event? Experiential activations are the perfect way to elevate the experience at your events. They create opportunities for them to sample products, purchase merchandise, and spread the word online for you! Experiential event activations are continuing to evolve and can be pretty amazing! Let those creative juices flow and discover something that amplifies the onsite experience. Experiential activations can also happen online through gamification—make it fun! Additionally, explore tools like interactive polling, word maps, and other ways to deepen the experience in live sessions - if the event is live streaming, include the online audience as well. Keep in mind that experiential marketing activations need to be tied to measurable outcomes.

EVENT GOALS NEED TO TRANSLATE TO THE DIGITAL SPACE

A live event cannot exist as an isolated moment; its impact must carry into the digital world where your audience continues to interact, engage, and convert. When you define event goals, start by identifying the measurable outcomes that will extend beyond the physical room. Are you aiming to increase email subscribers? Drive traffic to a specific offer? Capture user-generated content? Increase podcast downloads? Grow your LinkedIn audience? The goals you set inform not only the event design, but also how your team captures content, manages audience engagement, and facilitates post-event momentum. Every touchpoint — from stage presentations to breakout sessions to audience Q&A

— becomes strategic digital material that can fuel your brand long after the event ends. Your live event is the spark; your digital ecosystem is the engine that keeps the fire burning.

Determine What Measures Success

Success must be defined before the first attendee walks through the door. What does "winning" look like for this event? It may be the number of qualified leads generated, the revenue collected onsite, the depth of audience engagement, or the partnerships secured as a result of the experience. It may be social impressions, email sign-ups, content produced, or conversions into high-ticket programs. Clear definition of success metrics allows your team to track, evaluate, and optimize in real time. When you know what outcomes matter most, you can ensure that every moment of the event — every announcement, every call to action, every piece of content captured — moves you toward that goal. Success is not accidental. It happens through intentional, targeted and specific actions.

Contingency Planning

This is one of those situations where it is wise for you to plan for the worst possible outcomes. Excellence requires preparation, and preparation requires contingency. Live events can be full of unexpected twists, turns, and calamity — technology, timing, vendors, speakers, weather, travel — that demand a flexible, solution-focused mindset. Effective contingency planning is not about anticipating failure; it is about protecting the attendee experience at all costs. This includes having backup equipment, alternative run-of-show scenarios, additional staff who can step in, communication plans for unexpected delays, and clear decision-making authority among your team. When contingencies are in place, challenges become manageable, transitions feel seamless, and the audience never experiences the friction behind the scenes. The event remains polished, professional, and aligned with your brand standards, regardless of what happens.

Monitoring & FAQ

This is important because it sets the team members who are supporting you up for success. Events are fast-paced, and it is helpful to have a bank of approved responses and answers to frequently asked questions so response to attendees and those in the digital space can be quick and efficient. This also helps you ensure that the event CopySignature remains consistent and cohesive no matter who may be at the helm of your online presence.

Social Listening

Social listening transforms your event from a one-dimensional experience into a dynamic conversation. By monitoring hashtags, mentions, comments, and real-time reactions, you gain valuable insight into what resonates with your audience, what content is performing well, and where opportunities exist to amplify key moments. Social listening informs your communication strategy, allowing you to repost high-value content, spotlight attendees, address concerns instantly, and shape narratives that carry momentum long after the event concludes. When you actively listen to your audience, you honor their voices while strengthening your brand's relationship with them. The bottom line is, you and your team have to keep their digital ears to the ground.

Identifying Revenue-Generating Opportunities

Every event is filled with signals — the questions attendees ask, the sessions they engage with most, the challenges they express, the products they gravitate toward, and the content that sparks the most discussion. These signals are indicators of unmet needs and potential revenue streams. By observing patterns, capturing feedback, and analyzing behavior, you can identify opportunities to introduce new offers, refine existing ones, or develop entirely new revenue pathways. Events become fertile ground for innovation, revealing exactly what your audience is willing to invest in and how your expertise can serve them further.

Marketing Partner and Affiliates

Strategic partnerships elevate your event by increasing visibility, broadening reach, and enhancing attendee experience. Marketing partners, sponsors, and affiliates serve as amplifiers, introducing your event to audiences you may not reach on your own. Their participation adds credibility, resources, and promotional support that multiply your marketing impact. When aligned well, partners extend the life of your event, strengthen your messaging, and create mutually beneficial relationships that can be leveraged for future activations. Affiliates also incentivize shared promotion, generating buzz and supporting your sales goals without increasing your marketing workload.

WHEN THE CTA IS CASH, CREATE A SENSE OF URGENCY...YOU ORDER THEIR STEPS — CLOSE, AND CONVERT.

A strong call to action turns inspiration into commitment. When your CTA involves an investment — whether a program, product, or event — urgency must be rooted in clarity, not pressure. Your job is to illuminate the path forward, articulate the value, and guide attendees to the decision that aligns with their transformation. Scarcity should feel authentic. Urgency should feel justified. And the pathway should feel attainable. A powerful CTA is a form of leadership: you are helping your audience move closer to the outcome they desire, with the support and expertise that only you can provide.

Designing Social Media Offers That Drive Momentum

Social media surrounding your event should be designed to extend the energy of the room into the digital world. Your offers must be compelling enough to stop the scroll and irresistible enough to drive action. They should be time-bound, value-rich, and directly connected to the transformation your audience wants. This is where FOMO becomes a strategic tool — not as fear-based marketing, but as a reminder of the opportunities, breakthroughs, and outcomes happening inside your ecosystem. When crafted with intention, your social offers inspire action, deepen engagement, and convert energy into revenue.

Digital Marketing in The Real World

"Everything you do online should have a place to land in the real world."

~Tisha Holman

I call myself an "Analog Girl in a Digital World," and I know that there is an extension of your brand and digital marketing strategy that has to land and thrive in the real world. For serious-minded small business owners preparing to scale, you must embrace the fact that everything doesn't happen on the world wide web, and at some point, you must step out from behind the screen and allow your expertise to be experienced, witnessed, and validated in the spaces where people gather. Your digital presence is only as powerful as your real-world credibility.

For service-based businesses—especially expert-led brands—your thought leadership isn't just part of your marketing; it is the marketing. People hire people they trust, and organizations invest in experts whose voice carries weight and delivers results

Speaking engagements are one of the most effective, credibility-building assets you can add to your marketing ecosystem–they are proof of concept in motion. A stage gives you what an algorithm can't—undivided attention, a curated audience, immediate impact, and the ability to shape narrative in real time - powerful stuff, right?! Whether it's a corporate workshop, a conference keynote, a fireside chat, a university lecture, or a panel discussion, these opportunities position you as a trusted expert and thought-leader – wise and worth listening to. Speaking is about strategic positioning. Every stage you step on becomes a data point that reinforces your brand story, and an integral part of creating content that connects…and converts to cash.

There's a misconception that to land opportunities to speak on stages or earn press hits, you must already be well-known. The opposite is true because visibility is built through consistency, clarity, and confidence—celebrity is not the determining factor. The magnetic force of your CopySignature™, and keen understanding of your Perfect M.A.T.C.H.™ become assets that prepare you for bigger platforms–pieces of a puzzle that will catalyze a new level of exposure for your brand once you tap into it. It is your yellow brick road that leads to being booked and busy.

The digital world amplifies your voice; the real world amplifies your presence. Your job is to create synergy between the two.

Leveraging PR as a Growth Strategy

For a high-achieving, service-based business owner ready to scale, public relations is a strategic lever that elevates authority and accelerates growth. When approached intentionally, PR signals to the marketplace that your expertise is credible, trusted, and worthy of attention. Press placements legitimize your expertise in the eyes of potential clients, and communicate, without you ever having to say it, that your work carries weight.

The same principle applies to media and public relations. Press placements— whether long-form interviews, expert commentary, local news features, business publications, podcasts, or national outlets—act as third-party validation. Someone else deemed your expertise valuable enough to spotlight in front of an audience that trusts them. Someone else said, "They are the best solution to the problem you are facing as a business owner or executive." That kind of endorsement—especially from outlets your Perfect MATCH trusts— can shift perception in minutes. Public relations is a long-game though– it requires a level of patience and consistency. The pace of social media has contributed to misaligned expectations in the eyes of many small business owners who are looking for microwave results.

For example:

 - A strong digital strategy builds the reputation that gets you invited to the room.
- A strong stage presence creates the clips, soundbites, and insights that circulate online.
- A strong media profile increases your credibility, which makes you more appealing as a speaker.
- And each speaking gig or press opportunity drives new eyes back to your owned platforms

It's a visibility loop—and when you intentionally connect these pieces, it becomes the gift that keeps on giving.

Becoming Media-Ready

Being media-ready is about clarity, preparation, and the confidence to communicate with impact. The media values experts who can articulate their knowledge with ease, succinctness, and relevance. To succeed in this space, your CopySignature is going to be your best friend.

Clear Messaging

A media-ready entrepreneur knows exactly what they want to be known for. They have a well-defined topic stack, signature perspectives, and expert positioning language that reflects their CopySignature™. They can speak to their niche with authority and articulate their value quickly.

A Compelling Digital Footprint

Producers and editors conduct instant credibility checks. A well-designed, easy to navigate website, consistent social presence, and visible thought leadership reassure them that this is someone worth featuring. Notice I didn't say large numbers of followers, or celebrity status–they are looking for consistency.

Professional Press Materials

Every media-ready entrepreneur needs a media bio, high-quality headshot, clear speaking topics, and a media one-sheet. These assets form the infrastructure that makes them easy to book and easy to brief.

Soundbite Delivery

You need to be able to deliver clear, concise messaging in snackable soundbites. Be prepared to speak your language and reinforce what you have worked so hard to build integrating the CORE Model into your strategic approach.

Where to Begin When You're New to Press

If you have never pursued PR before, there is no time like the present for you to start to gain momentum; momentum that begins with strategic first steps.

Start Locally

Local outlets — news stations, community magazines, business journals — are often the most accessible place to begin. They welcome fresh voices and are eager for stories about entrepreneurship, impact, and local leadership.

Step Into Podcasts

Podcasts are one of the most powerful and underrated PR avenues. They allow for depth, nuance, and storytelling because they take you out of the "content hooks" and soundbites simply because they offer the gift of time in the conversation. Podcasts will help refine the talking points of your CopySignature, develop your delivery style, and create evergreen assets that build long-term authority. SCORE!

Provide Expert Commentary

Positioning yourself as an accessible expert source is the powerful show of credibility that brands in demand are built upon. Offering insight on industry trends, cultural conversations, or human-interest stories increases your visibility and builds trust with journalists and producers.

Cultivate Media Relationships

Media is built on relationships. Engaging with journalists and producers on social media channels like LinkedIn will help keep you top of mind when opportunities arise.

Master the Art of the Pitch

A strong pitch is precise, timely, and value oriented. It presents a clear angle that serves the outlet and positions the expert as a timely, relevant, newsworthy voice.

The best pitch answers a single question for the journalist:

"Why you, and why now?"

Run The Play!

PR Readiness Checklist

Are you prepared to show up as a credible, compelling, media-ready expert? Use this checklist to assess whether you're ready to pursue press and maximize the visibility it brings.

Brand Clarity

- I can clearly articulate who I am, what I do, and who I serve in one sentence.
- I have a defined point of view that differentiates me from others in my industry.
- My messaging is consistent across all platforms and aligns with my CopySignature™.
- I know the 3–5 signature topics I can speak on confidently and

repeatedly.

Digital Footprint

- My website is clean, current, and presents me as a credible expert.

- My social media profiles reflect professionalism, clarity, and thought leadership.

- My recent posts reinforce my expertise and offer valuable insight (not fluff).

- There is no outdated or contradictory content that weakens my authority.

Press Materials

- I have a polished, up-to-date media bio (long and short versions).

- I have high-quality headshots in multiple formats (vertical, horizontal, white background).

- I have a speaker/press one-sheet with my talking points and differentiators.

- I have a short list of "ready-to-go" interview questions I can answer with confidence.

If you feel you still have some work to do, reach out to a trusted public relations professional for help - it is worth the investment! In the meantime, check out my PRESS Pathway Framework as you continue to build in this area.

PRESS

PATHWAY

PREPARE YOUR PLATFORM

NOW YOU IDENTIFY WHY THE
MEDIA SHOULD CARE RIGHT NOW.

REFINE YOUR RELEVANCE

THIS IS WHERE YOU BUILD THE
FOUNDATION THAT MAKES YOU
BOOKABLE.

ENGAGE WITH GATEKEEPERS

THIS IS WHERE THE PITCHING AND
PLACEMENT BEGINS.

SECURE ALIGNED OPPORTUNITIES

VISIBILITY IS NOT A ONE-TIME EVENT
–IT'S AN ONGOING STRATEGY.

SUSTAIN & SCALE YOUR VISIBILITY

THIS IS THE RELATIONSHIP-
BUILDING PHASE.

The PRESS Pathway

Prepare Your Platform

- Establish brand clarity, messaging, and signature topics.
- Strengthen your digital footprint (website, social, content).
- Build foundational press materials (bio, headshot, one-sheet).
- Goal: Become a credible, discoverable expert.

Refine Your Relevance

- Craft timely angles, hooks, and stories.
- Connect your expertise to current trends or industry needs.
- Develop 5–7 go-to pitches based on value, not promotion.
- Goal: Position yourself as relevant, useful, and newsworthy.

Engage with Gatekeepers

- Research journalists, hosts, editors, and producers.
- Engage with their content (comment, share, support).
- Personalize outreach to show genuine alignment.
- Goal: Become a familiar, trust-worthy voice in their orbit.

Secure Aligned Opportunities

- Start with manageable outlets: podcasts, local news, niche publications.
- Pitch consistently using short, powerful, relevant angles.
- Respond to journalist callouts (HARO, Qwoted, social media requests).
- Goal: Stack small wins that lead to bigger platforms.

Sustain and Scale Your Visibility

- Repurpose press across all marketing channels.

- Add media logos to your website and social proof assets.

- Use past placements to attract higher-level opportunities.

- Track what works and refine your approach quarterly.

- Goal: Build a compounding media presence with long-term impact.

As you move into the next phase of your growth, remember that speaking and PR are not "extras" reserved for big companies or celebrity entrepreneurs. They are practical, strategic tools available to you right now. Tools that can transform the way your audience perceives you. Tools that anchor your authority, expand your reach, and elevate your brand beyond what an algorithm could ever deliver.

Let this chapter be your permission slip to step out from behind the comfort of your content calendar and into the rooms where leaders are made. Your voice, your story, and your expertise deserve to be heard—not just online, but everywhere your ideal clients gather. Your expertise shouldn't live in a vacuum. It's meant to be shared, taught, demonstrated, and amplified.

Unlikely Mentor:
After Action Reviews (AAR)
Military Precision in Evaluation

In the military, After Action Reviews (AARs) are conducted after every mission — whether it was a success or a failure. This process happens without blame or ego because the goal is learning fast, adapting faster, and ensuring no mistake is repeated.

The process is simple but powerful:

1. What was supposed to happen?
2. What actually happened?
3. Why were there differences?
4. What will we do next time to improve?

The Lesson: Measure Without Ego

The AAR model shows that evaluation must be:

- Objective: Facts, not feelings.
- Regular: Not just when there's a crisis.
- Actionable: Clear decisions about what changes moving forward.

Questions

- What are you measuring right now that makes you feel good but doesn't truly reflect progress?
- Where are you avoiding data because you fear what it might reveal?
- How will you know when it's time to evolve or pivot?

 **Run The Play!**

1. Set 3 Non-Negotiable KPIs: Choose metrics that reflect business health, not vanity numbers.
2. Conduct a Quarterly Business Review: Analyze wins, misses, and opportunities every 90 days.
3. Create a Feedback Loop: Implement a simple, consistent way to gather client or audience feedback.

Pulling it all Together

Bringing It All Together:
Your Next Era Starts Here

You've reached the final pages of this playbook — but what you're stepping into now is not an ending. It's the beginning of a new era for your business, your voice, and your leadership.

You now understand what most entrepreneurs never discover: sustainable digital success isn't built on trends, hacks, or nonstop hustling. It's built on clarity, systems, alignment, and intentional execution. It's built by leaders who turn strategy into structure, structure into action, and action into momentum.

Throughout this book, you haven't been collecting concepts — you've been building your ecosystem. You now possess the complete architecture for a business that moves with rhythm, purpose, and predictability. A business where:

✓ **Your message is unmistakable** because CopySignature™ gave it shape and soul.

✓ **Your audience is aligned** because Perfect M.A.T.C.H.™ clarified who you're truly here to serve

✓ **Your operations support excellence** because C.O.R.E.™ grounded you in stability and scalability.

✓ **Your goals are structured and strategic** because S.C.A.L.E.™ gave you a framework for growth.

✓ **Your marketing has a roadmap** because STAGE™ organized your execution and distribution.

✓ **Your revenue streams are intentional** because the P.O.T. of Gold™ revealed where the expansion truly lives.

✓ **Your visibility is elevated and expanding** because the PRESS™ Framework positioned you for authority, media, and real-world reach.

You can close this book and go back to business as usual — busy but unfocused, creating but not converting, visible but not positioned. Or you can decide, right now, that this is the moment everything changes. The moment you stop operating from uncertainty and start operating from strategy. The moment you stop waiting for the perfect timing and start building the future your brand deserves. The marketplace isn't waiting for the most talented entrepreneur — it rewards the most prepared, the most consistent, the most strategic, and the most visible.

It rewards the leader who:

- Builds systems instead of stress.
- Speaks with authority instead of hesitation.
- Creates aligned offers instead of random ones.

- Pursues visibility through PRESS™ instead of passively hoping to be discovered.
- Treats their marketing as an ecosystem instead of an afterthought.

That leader is now you.

You've gained the clarity.

You've learned the systems.

You've built the language.

You've identified the audience.

You've mapped the strategy.

You've uncovered the revenue pathways.

You've established the visibility roadmap.

Everything you need to build a profitable, recognizable, and scalable digital presence is already within your reach. The question is no longer how. You have the answers.

The question is ***when.***

When will you stop shrinking and start leading?

When will you step into the authority you've earned?

When will you trust the frameworks you now possess?

When will you show up consistently enough for the market to feel your impact?

When will you pursue PRESS™, stages, and real-world visibility with intention?

When will you decide to become the undeniable voice in your industry?

You didn't pick up this book by accident. You picked it up because something inside you knew there was more for your brand, more for your message, and more for the people you're called to serve. You're not just building a business — you're building a legacy. A body of work and a presence that will outlive algorithms, trends, and shiny new platforms.

As you step into this next chapter of your growth, remember that transformation happens in layers. You are not the same person who opened this book. You are more informed, more equipped, and more aligned. But most importantly — you are now responsible for the knowledge you hold.

Your business will grow to the level of your execution.
Your brand will rise to the level of your visibility.
Your impact will expand to the level of your courage.

This is your moment to build what you've always imagined.
 Not later. Not someday. Now.

It's time for you to start to Mind Your Business.

Your Next Steps

Ground Yourself in C.O.R.E.™

Stabilize your foundation.

- Clarify your messaging, offers, systems, and processes.
- Audit your operations for gaps, bottlenecks, or inefficiencies.
- Ensure your internal structure can support the growth you want.

YOUR BUSINESS CAN'T SCALE WHAT ISN'T STABLE.

Refine Your Audience with Perfect M.A.T.C.H.™

Re-align who you serve and why.

- Re-evaluate your ideal client using the MATCH criteria.
- Update your personas, pathways, and content focus.
- Refine your brand and messaging to speak directly to that person.

ALIGNMENT CREATES MOMENTUM.

Strengthen Your Message with CopySignature™

Shape the voice you want to be known for.

- Finalize your core messaging pillars.
- Create signature stories, examples, and soundbites.
- Rewrite your web copy, scripts, and email flows using your CopySignature.

MESSAGING IS YOUR MAGNET.

Build or Refine Your Offers with the P.O.T. of Gold

Expand your revenue and impact.

- Identify which products, opportunities, and treasures you already have.
- Map the gaps: What needs to be created? What can be optimized?
- Prioritize the revenue streams that align with your long-term vision.

Your gold is already in your business — uncover it

Build Your Marketing Engine with STAGE™

Turn strategy into movement.

- Map out your content, assets, campaigns, and visibility plan.
- Choose your platforms based on audience, not preference.
- Build your distribution rhythm (daily, weekly, monthly touchpoints).

Consistency is the multiplier.

Elevate Your Visibility with PRESS™

Move from seen to sought after.

- Prepare your press materials (media bio, headshots, one-sheet)
- Build your story bank and angle library.
- Begin pitching podcasts, local media, online publications, or industry outlets.
- Track and repurpose every placement for maximum reach.

Visibility is the fastest path to authority.

Set Your Goals with S.C.A.L.E.™

Create goals you can execute.

- Define Strategy-Aligned goals.

- Ensure they are Client-Centric and tied to revenue.
- Break them down into Actionable, Automated, Leveraged, Expert-Reinforcing steps.
- Review and refine them quarterly.

Goals without structure are just wishes.

Measure & Iterate with Evaluate & Elevate

Your growth is in your data.

- Track performance across marketing, operations, and visibility.
- Identify what's working and what needs recalibrating.
- Adjust based on data, not emotion.

What gets measured gets done.

The 10 Laws of
Digital Marketing

The 10 Laws of
Digital Marketing Power

The 48 Laws of Power is a New York Times Best Seller written by Robert Greene. The book gets a bad rep because it is seen as being a manipulative and deceptive tool leveraged as a means to achieve power If we are honest, marketing is manipulation too– it is just the positive side of it–kind of like the devil and the angel that pop up on your shoulder when you are at the crossroads of a big decision. The psychology of branding and marketing can sometimes be dark; It is all about perspective. Step into the dark side with me and use your powers for good to build a legacy brand that fulfills your purpose, brings you joy, and positions you for profits.

ONE

Lead With Strategy

Growth is never the result of random acts of marketing. It is the product of an intentional strategy that guides every decision, platform, and investment. When businesses begin with tactics instead of strategy, they create disjointed efforts that are difficult to sustain or measure. True digital leadership begins with a clearly defined blueprint that connects marketing activities directly to revenue and brand equity.

TWO

Build A Brand That's In Demand

Your brand is not just a visual identity; it is the sum of the experiences, messaging, and trust signals you create. Without strong positioning, your brand blends into the noise of competitors. By defining a unique market position and consistently reinforcing it across every touchpoint, you establish authority and create differentiation that makes competition irrelevant.

THREE

Community Is The New Currency

Platforms you do not control — social media accounts, ad platforms, third-party groups — can never be fully relied upon for long-term stability. Building a foundation of owned assets, such as email lists, private communities, and branded platforms, protects your reach and ensures that your audience connection cannot be disrupted by algorithm changes or platform policies.

FOUR

Monetize With Intention

Revenue growth is not a matter of chance. It requires carefully designed offers that move clients through a value ladder, creating increasing levels of transformation and investment. When revenue is engineered with intention, marketing efforts become predictable, measurable, and directly tied to financial outcomes rather than one-off wins.

FIVE

Align Every Goal With Strategy

Growth without alignment leads to wasted resources and scattered energy. Every goal must trace directly back to your core strategy — not just what you could do, but what you must do to move the business forward. When goals are strategy-aligned, every action creates compounding results rather than one-off wins.

SIX

Master Magnetic Messaging

Your messaging must bridge the gap between what you offer and what your audience desires most. Clear, compelling language is not optional — it is the mechanism that moves potential clients from awareness to action. By deeply understanding your audience and aligning messaging with their values and aspirations, you create communication that drives conversion and loyalty.

SEVEN

Integrate Tech To Create Efficiency

Technology should serve as the operational backbone of your marketing efforts. Ethical AI, automation, and integrated platforms allow teams to reduce manual work, streamline processes, and focus on high-value activities. The goal is not to replace human creativity but to create systems that increase speed and precision without sacrificing connection or authenticity.

EIGHT

Measure What Matters

The strongest brands are making data-driven strategic decisions. Vanity metrics like likes and followers create the illusion of progress but rarely connect to actual growth. Businesses must define meaningful KPIs and establish regular evaluation rhythms that inform decisions, optimize performance, and eliminate wasted effort.

NINE

Protect Your Brilliance

Your frameworks, content, and client experiences are core assets of your business. Without proactive protection through trademarks, copyrights, and brand guidelines, these assets are vulnerable to imitation or misuse. Safeguarding your intellectual property is critical to sustaining competitive advantage and preserving the integrity of your reputation.

TEN

Play The Long Game

Short-term tactics may create spikes in visibility or revenue, but they rarely translate into lasting success. Sustainable growth comes from building assets, processes, and relationships that compound over time. This approach requires patience, consistency, and a long-term vision for the impact your business will have in the market.

ABOUT THE AUTHOR

Tisha Holman, PMP, is the Founder and CEO of Mind Your Business, LLC. She is a highly sought after digital marketing, brand, and social media strategist who has helped organizations large and small implement strategies to elevate their digital presence. She is an industry expert dedicated to sharing knowledge that helps organizations from all industries solidify the foundation their businesses are built upon, and win in the digital marketing space. Tisha is a Sacramento, CA native, and a graduate of California State University, Sacramento with a Bachelor of Arts degree in Communication Studies. She served as the Chair of the Membership & Marketing Committee for the Sacramento Urban League, and was awarded the "Top 30 Under 30" Award by the Sacramento Observer. Tisha has been at the helm of national digital marketing campaigns that were aired on Lifetime Television, TBN, Daystar Television, The Word Network, ABC, NBC, and more! She developed the digital and social media campaigns that helped T.D. Jakes' book, SOAR!: Build Your Vision From The Ground Up, rise to the top of the New York Times Best Sellers list, and the movie "Faith Under Fire: The Antoinette Tuff Story" premier with record-breaking ratings. Tisha has been featured on ABC, CBS, FOX, and The CW, and has spoken on domestic and international stages, sharing her insights and expertise.

Now a resident of Houston, TX, in her spare time, Tisha enjoys great food, travel, live music, and the arts. Tisha serves on the Brand Awareness Committee of the YMCA of Greater Houston and is a member of the National Coalition of 100 Black Women, Houston Metropolitan chapter. Her greatest accomplishment is her daughter, Sydney Alexandria—a truly amazing young lady, brilliant, kind, and beautiful inside and out.

Tisha is the host of The Well-Rounded Podcast, Author of Lights! Camera! Action!: Get Your Brand on Television, The Social Media Makeover 2nd Edition, Go Ye Into All The World Wide Web, The Digital Marketing Strategy Playbook, and the Creator of The Digital Day Planner and Business Scents.

* 9 7 9 8 2 1 8 8 8 3 4 3 0 *